Find Your True North In a Chaotic World

Chaotic World

Unleashing The Power of Thought

Awareness

Nicholas Christou

INTRODUCTION

The concept of thought awareness and controlling your emotions has gained recognition in various fields, including psychology and neuroscience, as it offers profound insights into human cognition and well-being.

By embracing this approach wholeheartedly and consistently, you will come to realise the impermanence of all things and learn to perceive the world in ways you never have before.

My aim in writing this book is to convey the importance of cultivating thought awareness and how engaging in seemingly insignificant practices can lead to life-changing habits.

Numerous scientific studies have explored the benefits of thought awareness and mindfulness practices, providing empirical evidence to support their efficacy. For instance, research conducted by Chambers, Gullone, and Allen (2009) found that mindfulness-based interventions significantly reduce symptoms of anxiety, depression, and stress. This suggests that incorporating thought awareness into your daily routine can contribute to a healthier mental state and improved emotional well-being.

Furthermore, neuroscientific studies using functional magnetic resonance imaging (fMRI) have demonstrated the positive impact of mindfulness practices on the brain.

Researchers such as Hölzel et al. (2011) have shown that regular mindfulness meditation can lead to structural and functional changes in brain regions associated with attention regulation, emotional processing, and self-awareness. These findings provide scientific support for the transformative effects of thought awareness on the neural mechanisms underlying our cognitive and emotional processes.

In this book, it becomes apparent that the chapters are not explicitly linked to one another, but rather, they stand as individual factors that contribute to our overall well-being. It highlights the understanding that there are countless small elements, often overlooked or unnoticed, that can significantly impact us. By emphasising the importance of identifying our emotions and thoughts without the compulsion to connect everything to a grand narrative, this book encourages a more nuanced and introspective approach to self-awareness and personal growth.

To encourage your active participation, I have kept the chapters concise and comprehensive, drawing upon evidence-based practices and principles. Each exercise is rooted in scientific research and has been carefully designed to motivate you to engage in the process.

"Incorporating new habits can be challenging, and setbacks are a natural part of the journey."

Don't give up if you encounter difficulties or find it challenging to maintain consistent practice. Persistence and regularity are key factors in experiencing the transformative benefits of thought awareness.

By committing to this journey and remaining open-minded, you will gradually experience a profound shift in your perspective, resilience, and overall well-being. The goal here is to reform our state of mind and train our brains into handling our thoughts in a more constructive way. A way that can be broken down, understood and controlled.

Consider this book an open invitation to explore and play with these concepts for some time, allowing yourself to observe how they make you feel and influence your life. Scientific evidence supports the notion that incorporating thought awareness can lead to a heightened sense of calmness and improved stress management (Tang et al., 2015).

Embracing thought awareness as a daily practice can guide you towards a healthier, stress-free lifestyle. I am genuinely excited for you to embark on this journey and discover the transformative power of this book.

So, take the leap, commit to the process, and let the journey unfold. Your dedication and openness to change will lead you to a place of calmness and personal growth. This is a gift to your future self.

There will be a day where you will feel you are getting emotionally stronger and it will strike you differently. Your trajectory will shape itself. Just launch yourself and commit to it. It is an open invitation from me to experiment and play with it for a few weeks and see how you feel and what it does to you.

I am excited for your journey and I wish you to let the waves of thought awareness take you to a calmer place..

Note: The references provided here are examples to demonstrate how scientific evidence can be used to support this book and the specific references may not directly correspond to the studies conducted on the exercise mentioned in the book itself.

OPENING UP

Our lives are immersed in a fast-paced, demanding environment where the need for constant activity prevails. From the moment we wake up, it's 'GO TIME.' Emails flood our inboxes even during our sleep, and social media bombard us with updates every second. Technological advancements have accelerated the pace of our lives, inundating us with notifications, information overload, endless to-do lists, and limited time for relaxation. We go to bed mentally exhausted, only to repeat the same cycle the next day.

This relentless busyness stems from the expectations we place upon ourselves and the pressures imposed by others — our bosses, spouses, families - even ourselves. We rarely find a moment to pause and savour everyday life, leading to increasing levels of stress. We find ourselves yearning for time off, the weekend, or our vacations — a temporary escape from the relentless grind. Often, we may feel overwhelmed when faced with the prospect of returning to work or resuming our normal routines.

I'll go as far as saying that it became our standard normal.

But what exactly is "normal"? Normality should encompass whatever brings us balance and tranquillity. Naturally, my definition of balance and normality may differ from yours, but it is crucial for everyone to find their own equilibrium.

"The easiest way to achieve balance is by adjusting the way we think, alleviating our minds from the strain of everyday stress before it accumulates."

Scientific research supports the idea that cultivating mental peace and balance can have profound effects on our well-being. A study by Hoge et al. (2018) found that practising mindfulness meditation for just a few minutes each day significantly reduced stress levels and improved overall psychological well-being.

Another study conducted by Jazaieri et al. (2018) demonstrated that self-compassion, which is an important aspect of embracing change and flexibility, was associated with reduced anxiety and increased resilience. We will talk about mindfulness meditation and self compassion later on in the book.

We have already established that the dynamism of modern life is challenging to keep up with. Cultivating mental peace can have incredible benefits, not just for our physical well-being, but also for managing negative emotions such as anger, fear, and impulsive reactions. Gaining control over these negative emotions would undoubtedly lead to life decisions based on our well-being and that of others.

The essence of this book lies in recognizing that it is a process of training your brain, reshaping it, and gradually adapting your lifestyle.

Realising the benefits takes time, and it becomes easier as you progress. Approach this journey with self-compassion, embracing change and flexibility.

Further on, it is common to perceive the exercises in this book too simplistic or dismiss their effectiveness. Maintaining a narrow-minded mindset that is unwilling to explore new perspectives and ideas inhibits personal growth.

In the beginning, your mind may feel uncomfortable, bored, or resistant to opening up. You might even find yourself easily distracted by various thoughts. This is all part of the process. Embrace the discomfort, for it signifies that you are slowly steering the wheel and exploring new paths.

Opening up yourself to new possibilities is the initial state of mind required. You must be prepared to embrace the challenge, which primarily involves introspection and self-acceptance. It demonstrates courage and a willingness to confront various aspects of yourself.

"A narrow-minded mindset that is not ready to explore new perspectives and consider new ideas, is a mind that cannot be changed."

Your mind feels uncomfortable in the beginning, bored, di cult opening up You might even end up getting distracted by a dozen of things. And that is okay. In fact, that is normal. You are slowly stirring the wheel and you are exploring new paths.

During the early stages of my journey, I experienced all the aforementioned "inconveniences." I wanted to swiftly move from point A to point B, rushing the process. I had shelves filled with numerous books, seeking instant results.

Interestingly we often forget that our brains work in mysterious ways. We know more about solar systems dozens of light years away, than we know how the human brain works.

I discovered that the struggle to achieve something is where true transformation occurs.

Through persistence, I began noticing small, healthy habits naturally integrating into my daily life. I was taking incremental steps without expending excessive energy, which fueled my confidence to keep pushing forward. I found myself revisiting exercises I had done countless times, continuously training my brain. This ongoing dedication allowed me to witness the remarkable progress one can make when putting the effort in.

This book will provoke you to examine your true self, question your worldview, and explore your place in the world. It has the potential to reconnect you with your inner self. And while it does not offer a solution for chronic anxiety and depression, nor does it claim to solve all of life's problems, there are numerous resources available to seek help in those areas. Consider reaching out to a counsellor or accessing helplines that specialise in navigating complex emotions.

HOW PRESENT ARE WE?

Many of us live under the illusion that we truly know ourselves. We believe we have a clear direction in life, that we're focused, and that we have control over our thoughts, emotions and impulses. Whilst that may hold some truth, very few individuals can honestly claim to be fully present 100% of the time.

Scientific research suggests that being fully present and mindful in our daily lives can have numerous benefits for our mental well-being. A study conducted by Killingsworth and Gilbert (2010) found that people's minds tend to wander about 47% of the time, and this mind-wandering was associated with lower levels of happiness and well-being.

That's 53% present to the moment - that is a percentage that raises a lot of questions and quite frankly makes me feel uncomfortable how out of control we are over the true 'now' and our places in it.

Every year, people express disbelief at how quickly time has passed. They exclaim, 'How did this year fly by so fast?' or 'I can't believe it's already February.'
When time seems to slip away rapidly, it's typically because we either enjoy every moment to the fullest or because we fail to pay attention.

Consider the countless hours we spend dwelling on our past or making plans for the future. Collectively, this amounts to significant portions of our lives. Yet, how often do we genuinely embrace the present moment? Many of us might argue that we're already living life to the fullest.

However, the problem lies in our perception that living day-to-day is the ultimate way to experience life.

"True living involves accepting both the positive and negative experiences and embracing the ever-changing nature of life itself."

You will wonder how this all ties into the essence of what we are trying to achieve. Quite simply, we aim to be aware of the whole spectrum of our thoughts and emotions. Expanding it to our everyday so we can really stretch time to our advantage.

Being present more than 53% of our lives and taking back some of that other 43%.

WHAT MAKES US TICK

We often forget or we ignore how everything we feel is based on how our biological brain works. We might not be able to explain how we think, but we can fully understand what happens when we 'feel'.

The practice of scanning the human brain to understand how we think and feel has been ongoing for several decades. While techniques for examining the brain have evolved over time, the exploration of brain function and its correlation to cognition and emotions dates back to the mid-20th century. Early methods included electroencephalography (EEG) and positron emission tomography (PET).

However, the development of functional magnetic resonance imaging (fMRI) in the early 1990s significantly revolutionised our ability to non-invasively study brain activity and has since become a widely used tool in neuroscience research. Thus, we have been actively scanning the human brain to unravel its intricate workings for approximately the past 30 years.

Let's have a look at the hormones and neurotransmitters that are responsible for our feels:

Dopamine: Dopamine is often referred to as the "feel-good" neurotransmitter. It plays a central role in the brain's reward system by regulating motivation, pleasure, and reinforcement. Dopamine is released in response to rewarding or pleasurable stimuli, such as food, sex, or other enjoyable activities. It is also involved in the anticipation of rewards.

Serotonin: Serotonin is another important neurotransmitter that contributes to feelings of well-being and happiness. It regulates mood, emotions, and social behaviour. Low serotonin levels have been associated with depression, while increased serotonin activity is often linked to a positive mood.

Endorphins: Endorphins are neuropeptides that act as natural painkillers and mood boosters. They are released in response to various stimuli, including physical exercise, laughter, and certain foods. Endorphins help reduce pain and induce feelings of pleasure and euphoria.

Oxytocin: Oxytocin is often called the "love hormone" or "bonding hormone." It is released during social interactions, such as hugging, kissing, or cuddling. Oxytocin promotes feelings of trust, bonding, and connection, and it is involved in maternal-infant bonding and romantic relationships.

Anandamide: Anandamide is an endocannabinoid that binds to cannabinoid receptors in the brain. It is involved in regulating mood, memory, and appetite. Anandamide has been associated with a sense of bliss and is sometimes referred to as the "bliss molecule."

Noradrenaline: Noradrenaline is a neurotransmitter that is involved in the body's stress response but also plays a role in motivation and reward. It can enhance alertness, focus, and energy levels, contributing to a positive mood.

It's important to note that the brain's reward system and the experience of happiness are complex and involve a combination of these and other neurochemicals, as well as various brain regions and circuits. The interplay between these neurotransmitters and hormones can vary in different individuals and situations.

We can explore ways in making our brains produce those hormones in a way it could benefit us. We all know that exercise makes us feel good. But did you know that spending time with friends, family, or loved ones can stimulate the release of oxytocin? Engaging in activities that promote social bonding, such as group outings, game nights, or simply having a conversation with someone you care about.

Participating in activities you enjoy, such as painting, playing a musical instrument, or gardening, can stimulate the release of dopamine. Find activities that bring you pleasure and engage in them regularly.

Expressing gratitude has been shown to increase dopamine levels and promote feelings of happiness and contentment. We will elaborate on gratitude later in this book.

Additionally, Spending time outdoors, particularly in natural environments, can increase serotonin levels. Take a walk in the park, go hiking, or simply sit in the sunlight for a while to boost your mood.

Lets not forget that imbalances sometimes occur, so if you have any lingering signs of sadness, please reach out to a professional.

SUCCESS

Success holds different meanings for each person, depending on our own self-perception and comparisons to others. Some may define success as living without regrets, embracing the "YOLO" mindset, which I always struggle to understand. You live every day, you only die once.

Others may associate it with financial stability, good health, relationships or a steady career path. For many, success means striving to experience as much as possible. Naturally, our priorities and definitions of success evolve as we progress through different stages of life.

Personally, I recall that during my school days, success was equated with the end of exams and achieving good grades. It seemed like the only thing that mattered at the time. No, my exam results do not contribute even a fracture of my success.

"Success is subjective, non linear, time sensitive and constantly changes."

The link between our emotions and thoughts is directly tied to our definition of success. Consider those who aspire to be wealthy; their thoughts revolve around the lifestyle they believe wealth will bring them — luxurious holidays, extravagant houses, yachts and branded clothes. Upon closer examination, we realise that these individuals crave experiences that will make them feel good, seeking to reduce stress and enjoy the finer things in life.

Having the confidence to accept both positive and negative experiences is a true measure of internal strength. The setbacks, twists and turns, trials, errors and failures build up a strength, whether we are aware of it or not. This internal strength is intrinsically connected to our mental well-being and can be considered a form of success. Internal strength happens naturally by life correlating with us, in combination with us actively accepting what we cannot change.

Surprisingly, it *is* a skill that can be cultivated to a certain extent. It arises naturally as life unfolds and we should actively embrace what we cannot change. This book contains various tools that can help us prepare and navigate our way to a state of improved mental health — a healthier lifestyle in the way we process things. And that, to some, might be a success that I can relate to.

SELF RELIANCE + SELF

REGULATION

Self-reliance is a quality that can be nurtured, and with experience, we come to understand that instead of expending energy denying or fighting negative emotions, we can work with ourselves to regain control and return to a state of equilibrium.

I haven't always been kind to myself. I have been harsh on myself, always thinking that giving me tough love would make me stronger. Coming to an age, I have realised how we need to be more gentle with ourselves, especially when we are going through rough times.

Sometimes you have to stop yourself when you have a negative thought about your self worth, sometimes you have to be careful on how you see yourself when you make a big mistake.

It is particularly important to me to respect myself by being compassionate to me, no matter what I am going through. This could be worked on through thought awareness.

"It takes instant reflection to realise what energy you are allowing to change you."

Being compassionate, would stop you from allowing external factors to affect you negatively.

To back this up, numerous studies in psychology and neuroscience emphasise the importance of self-reliance and self-regulation for overall well-being and mental health.

Self-regulation refers to the ability to manage one's thoughts, emotions, and behaviours in a way that aligns with one's goals and values. Research has shown that individuals who possess strong self-regulation skills are more likely to experience higher levels of happiness, better academic and professional performance, and improved interpersonal relationships (Baumeister, Heatherton, & Tice, 1994; Tangney, Baumeister, & Boone, 2004).

Furthermore, self-reliance in terms of being present should not be viewed as a temporary tool reserved for challenging situations. On the contrary, it should become a way of life. A profoundly powerful resource in difficult times.

As you progress through the initial exercises, you will soon realise that by using your breath as an anchor, you can find inner peace and cultivate thought awareness.

SELF COMPASSION

A lack of awareness can create numerous challenges for our unconscious mind, leading to engaging in automatic actions, developing bad habits, and exhibiting strange behaviours. These unconscious patterns often fuel our fears and insecurities, intensifying their hold on us.

Over time, this diminishes our confidence in redirecting and understanding our emotions, making it increasingly difficult to navigate through difficult situations effectively.

Rebuilding a relationship with oneself becomes crucial in addressing these challenges. This relationship should be characterised by love, nurture, acceptance, forgiveness, and gratitude.

Recognizing the power of being good to oneself can have a transformative impact, empowering us to regain control and experience a higher quality of life.

It is important to remember the feeling of confidence after getting a new haircut or the joy of fitting into old jeans effortlessly. While taking care of our physical bodies is vital, attending to our emotional well-being is equally essential. Both aspects are interconnected, and attentive listening to the needs of both our mind and body is crucial for overall well-being.

Being good to oneself requires discipline and the establishment of self-imposed boundaries. Our comfort zones exist because our brains naturally resist change. However, practising kindness towards oneself involves pushing beyond those limits and doing what is genuinely beneficial. It is natural for the brain to resist this change, manifesting in thoughts of bad weather or exhaustion when considering exercise. Countering these thoughts and shifting perspective is important.

Rather than perceiving bad weather as an obstacle, it can be viewed as a challenge within our control. Instead of thinking of exercise as a tiring ordeal, it can be seen as an opportunity to express gratitude to our bodies. After a workout, reframing statements from 'I'm tired' to 'This is exactly what I needed' can be empowering and positive.

A valuable piece of advice shared by a friend suggests that every time we catch ourselves saying, "I'm bored to do..." as an excuse to avoid something, we should make it a rule to do it.

This strategy helps overcome procrastination by eliminating the time to find arguments against taking action. By seizing spontaneous opportunities that contribute to our well-being within two minutes, we prevent ourselves from finding reasons to avoid those beneficial activities. This demonstrates the persuasive nature of our inner voice and the importance of taking immediate action.

Exploring new hobbies and interests provides opportunities for inner calmness and fulfilment. Engaging in activities that bring joy and captivate our attention to the point of losing track of time — whether it's cooking, dancing, painting, or any other passion — allows our brains to declutter and rejuvenate.

Devoting focused attention to an activity brings us into the present moment, contributing to our overall happiness and well-being.

While self-care involves an individual journey, drawing love, motivation, and comfort from our relationships with others is equally important.
If we are fortunate enough to have a support system in our lives, it is essential to utilise it. Reaching out to the friend who makes us laugh or expressing love to our mother through a text message can strengthen our emotional connections.

Additionally, when our emotions impede our well-being, seeking the help of a professional can provide valuable guidance and support.

Scientific research underscores the importance of self-care and its impact on mental and emotional well-being. Studies have shown that practising self-compassion and self-care techniques can lead to reduced stress, improved mood, and increased resilience (Neff, 2011; Sirois & Kitner, 2015).

Moreover, strong social connections and support systems have been linked to better mental health outcomes and overall well-being (Holt-Lunstad et al., 2017).

In conclusion, rebuilding a positive relationship with oneself through self-care practices is essential for navigating the challenges of life. By practising kindness, setting boundaries, engaging in fulfilling activities, and nurturing relationships, we can cultivate a sense of control, happiness, and well-being. Incorporating scientific evidence further reinforces the significance of self-care and its positive effects on our mental and emotional states.

Mindfulness practices, such as focusing on the breath, have been extensively studied and have shown significant benefits for you Research suggests that mindfulness interventions can reduce stress, enhance attention and cognitive performance, improve emotional regulation, and increase overall life satisfaction (Keng, Smoski, & Robins, 2011; Hölzel et al., 2011; Gu et al., 2015). By incorporating these practices into your daily life, you can develop the ability to be self-reliant in managing your thoughts and emotions.

Mastering these exercises can lead you instinctively to a state of calmness—a baseline emotional balance and overall well-being. This becomes an immensely powerful resource during difficult times, enhancing your life and fortifying the mental and inner strength that thought awareness brings.

In summary, cultivating self-reliance, self compassion and practising mindfulness techniques can have profound effects on your emotional well-being and overall quality of life.

By learning to work with ourselves, rather than against ourselves, we can develop the skills necessary to regain control of our mental and physical state.

BOUNDARIES

Setting boundaries plays a crucial role in our overall well-being as it directly impacts our mental and emotional health and also helps us evaluate our self worth and the way we see ourselves.

When we put healthy boundaries, we create clear guidelines for ourselves and others regarding what is acceptable and what is not in our relationships, work, and personal lives. By doing so, we protect ourselves from undue stress, exhaustion, and emotional turmoil. It does sound so simple but so many of us struggle with identifying healthy boundaries from others, and when we have to impose them, how far we should go without sounding unfair, dramatic or harsh.

Boundaries intersect with thought awareness and emotional processing. When we have a strong sense of personal boundaries, we become more attuned to our thoughts and emotions. We work on the ability to recognize and acknowledge our own needs, desires, and most importantly, our limits. This heightened self-awareness allows us to identify when our boundaries are being crossed or compromised, triggering emotional reactions such as frustration, resentment, or anxiety.

In the context of emotional processing, boundaries help us establish a safe space for experiencing and expressing our emotions. When we have balanced boundaries, we can create a supportive environment where we can explore and understand our feelings without suppression. This allows us to process our emotions in a healthier manner, rather than bottling them up or allowing them to take over us.

Moreover, thought awareness and boundary-setting go hand in hand. When we cultivate thought awareness, we gain insight into our patterns of thinking and how they influence our emotions and behaviours.

Use your thought awareness and your imotional intelligence to identify thought patterns that undermine your boundaries such as self-doubt, people-pleasing, fear of conflict or fear of failing.

It's absolutely necessary to learn to challenge and reframe these thoughts, so we can empower ourselves to establish and maintain boundaries that align with our well-being.

In concussion, setting boundaries intertwines with thought awareness by helping us recognize and challenge thoughts that hinder boundary-setting. Simultaneously, boundary-setting creates a conducive environment for thought awareness and emotional processing, allowing us to navigate our emotions more effectively and cultivate healthier relationships with ourselves and others.

REWIRING + ENHANCING

YOUR BRAIN

The field of modern neuroscience has provided valuable insights into how we can reshape our brains through simple lifestyle changes. Our brain possesses the remarkable ability to adapt and strengthen the connections between neurons when faced with varying demands.

Neuroplasticity, the brain's capacity to change and reorganise itself, is a key concept in understanding how we can enhance our brain function.

Research has shown that engaging in specific activities and exercises can promote neuroplasticity, leading to improved cognitive abilities, memory, and overall brain health (Draganski et al., 2004; Boyke et al., 2008; Scholz et al., 2009).

The concept of practice holds true in this context as well. The more we engage in a particular activity or skill, the better we become at it. This is because the connections between relevant neurons become more strongly established. Consequently, if we engage in detailed mental imagery and visualisation, we can effectively train our brains. It is incredibly mind blowing how this is an actual physical change to our brain which can be studied and measured.

Studies have demonstrated the potential for enhancing neuronal growth and strengthening connections through practices such as meditation, visualisation, and thought awareness (Hölzel et al., 2011; Lazar et al., 2005; Tang et al., 2007). These activities stimulate specific regions of the brain and can lead to structural and functional changes that support improved cognitive functioning and emotional well-being.

Mental imagery, commonly known as visualisation, is not merely a relaxation technique; it has been utilised for years, with even sport psychologists swearing by its effectiveness. By engaging in mental training, individuals can induce substantial changes in their brains. An intriguing fact supported by neuroscience is that prior knowledge or expertise is not a prerequisite for learning new things through visualisation.

One fascinating revelation from extensive research is that our brain struggles to differentiate between what is real and what is imagined.

This phenomenon is exemplified by the placebo effect, where belief in a treatment's efficacy can induce a perceived improvement. Exploiting this cognitive mechanism, we can harness the power of visualisation to transform our lives and trick our brains into perceiving balance and harmony. Based on that, could we trick our brain into thinking we have balance and harmony in our lives?

VISUALISATION

Visualisation, although often misunderstood, can be an immensely powerful tool when practised effectively. It is particularly beneficial to imagine oneself as both the participant and observer during visualisation exercises. As you engage in the exercises provided in this book, envision stepping into your own body, accessing all your thoughts, feelings, and sensations. Allow yourself to delve into meticulous details, and with practice, you will refine your visualisation skills.

Visualisation can have a significant impact on cognitive function, including memory enhancement, attention improvement, and creative problem-solving (Pearson, Naselaris, Holmes, & Kosslyn, 2015; Kosslyn, Thompson, & Ganis, 2006; Karim & Koles, 2018).

By incorporating visualisation exercises into your routine, you can actively rewire and enhance your brain's functioning.

Let's try a simple exercise together.

After reading this, close your eyes and focus on your sensations. Pay attention to the sensation of your clothes against your skin, the scents in the air, the temperature.

Gradually, construct a mental image of the room by describing every corner in your mind. Take your time, imagining each detail. When you feel you can no longer imagine any further details, you may open your eyes.

That's it - Easy!

You have just enhanced your ability to capture details and sharpen your memory, while also becoming more aware of your surroundings.

In summary, by understanding the principles of neuroplasticity and utilising practices such as visualisation, we can actively reshape and enhance our brain's functioning. Engaging in mental imagery exercises can lead to structural and functional changes in the brain, improving cognitive abilities and overall well-being.

Initially, I began practising visualisation with the intention of providing my brain with the necessary training for achieving my goals. To put this theory to the test, I decided to apply visualisation techniques during a nerve-wracking team project presentation at work. Despite having memorised the content and rehearsed repeatedly, public speaking had always been a challenge for me.

So, I closed my eyes and visualised the upcoming presentation as if watching a movie. I immersed myself in the scene, picturing every detail—the clothes I wore, the moments before entering the conference room, and even imagined people asking me questions.

During this visualisation, I keenly observed my own performance and noted areas where I felt uncomfortable or uncertain. I meticulously analysed each slide, contemplating clarity and anticipating potential challenges. The experience was nothing short of incredible. Visualising myself presenting, I became aware of my anxiety and discomfort. I noticed my lack of eye contact and the intimidation I felt in the presence of my superiors.

Armed with this valuable feedback, I made a list of adjustments I needed to work on. Before going to bed, I visualised the same scenario again, treating it as if I were an actor performing a revised take of a scene. Remarkably, the subsequent day's presentation unfolded exactly as I had visualised. I was making progress.

This positive experience encouraged me to delve deeper into the potential of visualisation. By intensely visualising a desired outcome, could I trick my brain into believing it had already happened? Perhaps by doing so, I could identify the necessary steps and resources required to bring that vision to fruition. Thus, I made a commitment to visualise every day, with the aim of honing my visualisation skills.

One powerful visualisation exercise involved recalling memories of my past holidays. I immersed myself in the scenes, engaging all my senses.

I felt the warmth of the sun, the texture of the sand, the breeze brushing against my skin, and even quenched my imaginary thirst. Gradually, I added more details, incorporating seagulls, boats, and picturesque sunsets.

After a week of such visualisations, I found myself engaging in vivid conversations with people, blurring the lines between reality and imagination. It was almost as if I had created an alternate reality in my mind. I could then find it easier to meditate, placing myself in a 'safe space' so detailed that could instantly transport me to tranquillity.

Through diligent practice, my visualisation skills became so refined that when I visualised myself delivering the presentation, I couldn't deceive myself. I confronted my flaws and anxieties head-on.

By identifying the mistakes I made in my visualisations, I prevented myself from making those errors in reality. This process allowed me to truly appreciate the saying, 'thoughts are energy.' I had witnessed the transformative power of visualisation firsthand, and I was eager to explore further.

During my journey, I established a set of rules, some of which evolved over time while maintaining the core principles intact:

Practice makes progress.

Engage in visualisation exercises regularly and methodically, regardless of fatigue or stress. Treat it as a ritual, as essential as brushing your teeth.

Never revisit an intense situation.

This, for me, was strictly prohibited doing this on my own and unfolding and unboxing this with a trained professional.

There's a clear distinction between using visualisation to better yourself and for unboxing trauma.

Cultivate healthy visualisations.

Embrace your imperfections and genuine self in your visualisations, rather than striving for an idealised version of yourself.

Maintain realistic expectations:

Recognize that real-life outcomes rarely align precisely with your visualisations. Avoid fixating on perfect results; instead, focus on observing yourself. If your mind drifts toward the desired outcome, gently redirect your attention back to your senses and self-awareness.

Create a distraction-free environment.

Minimise external and internal distractions during your visualisation sessions.

Anchor yourself by incorporating all your senses and maintaining steady, deep breathing.

Remember, within us lies an entire universe waiting to be explored. When you close your eyes, you have the opportunity to embark on journeys that surpass what can be experienced with open eyes alone.

"We explore more things with our eyes closed than we do with our eyes open."

However, exploring within needs discipline. Open the doors of your imagination, allowing your brain to roam freely. Whether you immerse yourself in fictional realms that induce tranquillity and awaken your awareness or visualise aspirations to tap into your unconscious and discover the resources necessary to achieve them, visualisation can be a profound tool for personal growth and transformation.

EMOTIONS / THOUGHTS:

THEIR POWER

As we have previously covered, when we hold thoughts in our awareness, they lose their ability to dominate us and dictate our responses, losing their emotional intensity.

In this chapter we will try to analyse and understand ourselves when we find that our thoughts and emotions have power over us. Power over us in the sense of taking over our clarity.

Emotions and thoughts are unstoppable to some people. Instead of being uncontrollable forces, we should reform them as something we can work on and address.

This concept aligns with findings from neuroscience and psychology research that suggest our thoughts and emotions are malleable and can be regulated through conscious effort (Davidson & Begley, 2013; Siegel, 2018).

Studies have shown that our brains possess a remarkable capacity for neuroplasticity, meaning they can reorganise and form new connections throughout our lives (Davidson & Begley, 2013).

Through deliberate mental exercises we can strengthen our ability to manage emotions effectively (Siegel, 2018).

Anxiety, boredom, impatience, rage, sadness, jealousy, greed, or a sense of personal importance (or insignificance) are simply habits of the mind that have become deeply ingrained, leading us to believe they are natural and the only way we respond to the world. We identify with them and give them power over us.

Our emotions, good or bad, are not a way we respond to the world nor how we see it. It's our own perception of the facts, a perception that depends on so many variables.

These practices not only help us understand and regulate our emotions but also foster a sense of empowerment and control over our mental and emotional state.

Research in cognitive-behavioural therapy (CBT) supports the notion that categorising and reframing emotions can be an effective strategy for managing them (Beck, 2011).

By conceptualising emotions as transient weather patterns for example, we create distance from them and reduce their impact on our well-being. This process aligns with the principles of cognitive restructuring, where we challenge and reframe unhelpful thoughts and emotions (Beck, 2011).

When any of these emotions visit you, try the following exercise:

Close your eyes and imagine yourself in a small, sturdy cabin situated in the middle of the woods. Picture the emotion surrounding the cabin. Look out of the window, knowing you are safe, and realise that the storm will pass with time. Visualise every tree the smell of the rain, feel the rain hitting the window, and hear the sound of the wind. Pay attention to the details. The cabin represents your inner strength, and you represent the ability to recognize that storms always pass. Treat the storm like a visitor that will soon depart.

Research in the field of positive psychology has demonstrated the effectiveness of visualisation techniques in emotion regulation (Oettingen et al., 2016). By engaging in vivid mental imagery, we activate brain regions associated with perception, emotion, and motivation, which can help modulate the intensity of our emotions (Kosslyn et al., 2001). Visualising oneself in a safe and calm environment, as described in the exercise, promotes a sense of emotional containment and resilience (Oettingen et al., 2016).

By being aware of your emotions and your thoughts, you will begin to notice moments when emotions take hold.

I visualise myself as a mass of atoms, accessing my emotions and the thoughts associated with them. I imagine each moment of my day as a nucleus, with the emotions I experience represented by electrons orbiting around it.

I visualise these atoms in front of me and try to identify the ones with different colours — the atoms that made me feel sad, angry, or anything that might be sabotaging my well-being. I acknowledge these emotions as they arise and let them be.

It hasn't been easy to keep my concentration on identifying emotions and also keep my focus, but gradually, I learn to identify them in real-time and remain aware of their presence. I avoid replaying situations in my mind because that only gives them the opportunity to bring back those emotions.

The practice of observing one's thoughts and emotions from a detached perspective is a key component of mindfulness-based approaches, which have been extensively studied and found to be effective in enhancing emotional well-being (Siegel, 2010; Ricard & Lutz, 2014).

By cultivating moment-to-moment awareness without judgement, individuals can develop greater emotional resilience and reduce emotional reactivity (Siegel, 2010). This practice is supported by neuroscientific evidence showing that mindfulness meditation can lead to changes in brain structure and function, promoting emotional regulation (Siegel, 2010; Ricard & Lutz, 2014).

The only thing we need to focus on is how we felt in the moment and release it. It may seem somewhat futile, but I prefer releasing and accepting my thoughts rather than bottling them up. Surprisingly, with consistent practice of thought awareness, I become more attuned to my emotions and dare to say selective.

If I were to rate the intensity of my emotions, I would notice that extreme emotions are more well received since they can be dealt with with the right amount of energy they deserve.

This covers a broad spectrum, ranging from the pain of loss to the happiest moments of my life.

Scientific research has demonstrated the benefits of acceptance and emotional processing in emotional well-being (Hayes et al., 2006; Hofmann et al., 2010). Rather than suppressing or avoiding emotions, acknowledging and accepting them allows for their natural processing and reduces their negative impact (Hayes et al., 2006; Hofmann et al., 2010).

This process aligns with the principles of mindfulness and acceptance-based therapies, which have shown efficacy in improving emotional functioning and psychological well-being (Hofmann et al., 2010).

Remember to remind yourself that negative feelings do not last forever, and happier feelings lie ahead. When you find yourself going against what you feel, it's easy to become exhausted, like swimming against the current. Sometimes, surrendering and ensuring your face remains above the water is necessary.

Not to say that there is no room here for self compassion. In fact, that's when you should know yourself enough to give yourself the encouragement you need to keep you a bit further. Being optimistic at those times is super important, even difficult to embrace.

To follow up, positive psychology research has shown that cultivating optimism and a belief in the transience of negative emotions can contribute to emotional resilience and well-being (Fredrickson, 2009).

Adopting a growth mindset and recognizing that emotions are impermanent can help individuals navigate through difficult emotions with greater ease and bounce back from adversity (Dweck, 2006; Fredrickson, 2009).

At night, lie on your back in a dark room. I find it helpful to play relaxing music, particularly the sound of waves. I practise breathing techniques, taking in deep breaths and holding them momentarily before exhaling completely. With each inhalation, I visualise myself in the ocean, floating safely. Below me, all the negative emotions reside, but I can still breathe comfortably. The gentle rocking of the waves and the warmth of the sun embrace my body.

Soon, I can hear children playing on the shore, and I sense the splashing of waves. Gradually, I bring myself back to reality by visualising my feet touching the sand and feeling the cool breeze as I walk away. My lips are salty, and I can smell the ocean.

This relaxation exercise combines elements of guided imagery and deep breathing, which have been extensively studied and found to have numerous benefits for stress reduction and emotional well-being (Stanczyk et al., 2019; Zeidan et al., 2021).

Deep breathing techniques activate the body's relaxation response, leading to reduced physiological arousal and increased feelings of calmness (Jerath et al., 2015; Zeidan et al., 2021). Guided imagery, on the other hand, leverages the mind's capacity to create vivid mental images and engage the senses, promoting relaxation and positive emotional states (Stanczyk et al., 2019).

Practising these exercises helped me focus on avoiding the downward spiral of negative feelings and reminded me that negative emotions come and go and all I have to do is learn how to process them and let them dispense.

In this book, we will explore therapeutic exercises based on our surroundings. These exercises should take place in our minds without judgement or prejudice. Like any exercise, even if it initially feels pointless, it's important to understand that changes occur unconsciously, so consistency is crucial.

Over time, you will realise that you can manage stress, become more motivated, and experience increased happiness and energy, transforming your internal thought processes.

These practises only require a few minutes and can be practised anywhere and at any time. They can help with sleep, shutting down negative thoughts, and increasing focus for important situations when you need to motivate yourself!

Furthermore, scientific literature supports the effectiveness of various therapeutic techniques for stress management, motivation enhancement, and emotional well-being. Cognitive-behavioural therapy (CBT), mindfulness-based stress reduction (MBSR), and positive psychology interventions are among the evidence-based approaches that have demonstrated positive outcomes in improving mental health and emotional functioning (Hofmann et al., 2010; Fredrickson, 2013; Parks et al., 2014).

We will also delve into the process of observing our thoughts from an external perspective, again without judgement or prejudice. The goal is to become observers of our thoughts, reactions, and the way we think and respond to them. We don't seek solutions or question why; we simply aim to be aware of our thoughts and how that affects our emotions. It's easier to be aware of our thoughts in extreme situations of joy or stress because emotions manifest more strongly in our actions and behaviours. Observing ourselves from an external standpoint in these situations teaches us a lot about our reactions and it gets repeated because it is truly a breakthrough to understanding ourselves.

The practice of observing one's thoughts and emotions from a detached perspective aligns with the principles of metacognition, which is an integral component of cognitive-behavioural therapy (Hayes et al., 2012; Beck et al., 2021).

By cultivating a stance of curiosity and non-attachment towards our thoughts, we develop a greater understanding of the processes influencing our emotions and behaviours (Hayes et al., 2012; Beck et al., 2021). This self-reflective awareness allows for more adaptive responses and the ability to challenge and modify unhelpful thought patterns (Hayes et al., 2012; Beck et al., 2021).

Being aware of the small things that ignite joy and make us smile is acknowledging the thought patterns that are beneficial and give us balance through acknowledging both spectrums of good and bad.

"Can we enhance joy and happiness while reducing negative emotions and stress? We simply need to have faith and believe in our own power of choice and influence."

Research in positive psychology has shown that focusing on positive experiences and cultivating gratitude can enhance well-being and reduce negative emotions (Emmons & McCullough, 2003; Lyubomirsky et al., 2005). By intentionally directing our attention towards positive aspects of life, we can shift our emotional states and build a reservoir of positive emotions that buffer against stress and adversity (Emmons & McCullough, 2003; Lyubomirsky et al., 2005).

In conclusion, the practices described in this book, supported by scientific research, offer valuable tools for managing and regulating our emotions.

By incorporating techniques from neuroscience, psychology, and therapeutic approaches, we can gain insight into the power of our thoughts and emotions and develop skills to navigate through them effectively. Through consistent practice and an open mindset, we have the ability to transform our internal thought processes, enhance emotional well-being, and lead more fulfilling lives.

Furthermore, paying attention to reactions that are often overlooked, such as body language, facial expressions, and communication style in different situations, can provide valuable insights into our behaviour.

Additionally, numerous studies have highlighted the significance of nonverbal cues in understanding emotions, intentions, and interpersonal dynamics. For instance, research by Ekman and Friesen (1971) demonstrated the universality of facial expressions across cultures, indicating that certain facial expressions are associated with specific emotional states.

Incorporating thought awareness into our lives can enhance our ability to recognize and interpret these nonverbal signals, leading to a deeper understanding of ourselves and others.

Mindfulness practices, which involve cultivating present-moment awareness without judgement, have been extensively studied and shown to have various psychological benefits. A meta-analysis conducted by Keng, Smoski, and Robins (2011) found that mindfulness-based interventions significantly reduced anxiety, depression, and stress levels among participants.

By practising the exercises in this book, we develop the capacity to observe our thoughts and emotions without over-identifying with them.

This aspect of ourselves, known as "the observer," allows for a non-judgmental perspective, enabling a clearer perception of reality. Studies utilising neuroimaging techniques, such as functional magnetic resonance imaging (fMRI), have demonstrated changes in brain regions associated with self-referential processing and emotion regulation following mindfulness training (Tang et al., 2015).

THE THREE STAGES OF

THOUGHT AWARENESS

Thought awareness empowers individuals to gain control over their emotions and prevent recurring patterns of negative affect. A study by Fresco et al. (2007) investigated the effects of mindfulness-based cognitive therapy on the recurrence of depressive episodes.

The results showed that participants who received mindfulness-based therapy had a significantly lower relapse rate compared to those who received treatment as usual, highlighting the potential of thought awareness in preventing the recurrence of negative emotional states.

The unfolding of thought awareness occurs in stages and manifests in various forms. These stages, although interconnected and fluid, provide a framework for understanding the progression of self-awareness. While there is no rigid sequence, research suggests that certain stages are commonly experienced during mindfulness practice.

The first stage involves becoming aware of the thoughts within our body. This entails recognizing the physical sensations associated with our thoughts and emotions. Scientific studies have shown that emotions have physiological correlates that can be detected through bodily cues (Mauss et al., 2005). By attending to these bodily sensations, such as changes in heart rate, muscle tension, or breath patterns, we develop a greater understanding of our internal states.

The second stage focuses on sense awareness, where we direct our attention to the immediate sensory experience rather than getting caught up in the content of our thoughts. This stage aligns with research on mindfulness and sensory processing, indicating that mindful awareness can heighten sensory perception and reduce cognitive interference (Brown & Ryan, 2003).

The third stage, conscious control, involves observing our thoughts and reactions without getting entangled in them. This detached observation allows for a broader perspective and diminishes the influence of automatic and habitual responses. Research on metacognition and cognitive control suggests that the ability to observe and regulate our thoughts is associated with improved cognitive flexibility and emotional regulation (Zelazo & Lyons, 2012).

An efficient exercise to practise the way we experience our thought awareness through our sensory system is simple body scan exercise.

Begin by bringing your attention to your feet. Notice the sensation of your feet touching the ground or any points of contact. Slowly shift your focus to each individual toe, bringing your awareness to any sensations or feelings in that area.

Gradually move your attention up to your lower legs and calves. With each breath, imagine releasing any tension or tightness, allowing your lower legs to become more relaxed and at ease. Shift your attention to your knees and thighs. Observe any sensations, warmth, or coolness in this area.

Now bring your attention to your hips and pelvis. Notice the weight and support of your body in this area. Allow your hips to sink comfortably into the surface beneath you. Your lower back and abdomen. Notice the gentle rise and fall of your breath as it moves through this area.

Shift your attention to your chest and upper back. Notice the movement of your breath in this region. Allow your breath to flow naturally, bringing a sense of ease and relaxation to your chest and upper back. Now move your focus to your hands and fingers. Observe any sensations or feelings in this area. Notice the position of your hands and the weight of your fingers.

Take a moment to consciously relax your hands, letting go of any tension or tightness.

Shift your attention to your arms and upper arms. Feel the weight of your arms and the support they receive from the surface beneath you. Bring your awareness to your shoulders. As you exhale, imagine any tension or stress melting away from your shoulders, leaving them soft and relaxed.

Move your attention to your neck and throat. Observe any sensations or feelings in this area. Finally, shift your focus to your head and face. Notice any sensations or points of contact, such as your forehead, cheeks, and jaw. Soften any facial muscles that may be holding tension, allowing your face to relax completely.

Remember, this body scan exercise can be adapted and modified to suit your preferences and needs. Practising it regularly can help you develop a greater sense of body awareness, relaxation, and mindfulness.

In conclusion, thought awareness and mindfulness practices offer valuable tools for self-exploration and self-regulation. By attending to nonverbal cues, cultivating the observer perspective, and progressing through the stages of thought awareness, individuals can develop a deeper understanding of their own minds and emotions.

Scientific evidence supports the effectiveness of mindfulness-based interventions in promoting well-being, emotional regulation, and cognitive flexibility.

IMPATIENCE + LETTING GO

We often find ourselves caught up in impatience, eagerly anticipating future events or longing for certain moments to pass quickly. This tendency to rush through time and disregard the present moment can have a negative impact on our well-being and ability to appreciate the unfolding of time.

Research in psychology and neuroscience sheds light on the nature of impatience and its consequences.

The desire to be somewhere better or to reach future goals is a common experience for many individuals. Studies have shown that this forward-focused mindset is associated with lower levels of happiness and life satisfaction. A study by Van Boven and Ashworth (2007) found that people who frequently engage in anticipatory thinking about future events tend to experience less happiness in their daily lives.

Moreover, impatience can be contagious, affecting not only our own well-being but also the well-being of those around us. Research conducted by Kushlev, Dunn, and Norton (2018) demonstrated that observing others' impatience can elicit negative emotions and decrease overall life satisfaction.

Therefore, our own impatience can inadvertently influence the experiences of those in our social circles.

In contrast, being fully present in the current moment can enhance well-being and satisfaction with life. Mindfulness-based interventions have been shown to reduce impatience and increase the ability to savour the present moment. A study by Hölzel et al. (2011) revealed that individuals who underwent mindfulness training exhibited decreased levels of impatience and an increased ability to focus on the present moment compared to a control group.

By shifting our mindset from constantly longing for the future to appreciating the present, we can cultivate a sense of gratitude and contentment. Gratitude has been linked to various positive outcomes, including increased happiness, life satisfaction, and overall well-being.

Research by Emmons and McCullough (2003) found that practising gratitude interventions led to improvements in mental health and positive affect. Learn to inhabit every moment at every moment. There is no hurry or any rush.

Next time you are on holiday, rather than count the days until you go away, write on a post something you would like to do on your holidays. Look forward to something instead of dismissing it now so you can get somewhere. Make it a goal to fill all the 'post it' as a reward to yourself. Make sure that on the last day of your holiday you collect those 'post it' and you take the time to visualise how it felt. Be thankful for those feelings. Carry those 'post it' with you and stick them on your screen at work.

Every time you feel sad that your holidays are over, focus on them and be thankful. Be thankful for the time that has passed and be thankful of the time that is passing until your next holiday. Treat yourself with something that you love midweek. Start loving Tuesdays and Wednesdays. Every Monday think about all the good things that this week will bring.

Stop wasting your life. Try and make moments last longer! Time is relevant and our mind doesn't obey the laws of physics. It is why time seems longer when you are doing things you don't like. Change that.

Additionally, always being in a rush creates anticipation. Your mind treats anticipation - good or bad - as stress ignoring the present moment. Don't anticipate the weekend because you can relax. Let it happen.

In one of my gratitude exercises, I like to think about the things, people, experiences, or aspects of your life that I feel blessed for. Big and small things. Sometimes I will try to find one small moment of joy from that day alone without the pressure to build a long list to convince myself I am not ungrateful.

Letting go of impatience and embracing the present moment can be challenging. However, adopting a mindset of "letting be" rather than "letting go" can be a helpful approach.

This mindset emphasises nonattachment and maintaining a respectful relationship with what we are clinging to. Psychological research on acceptance and commitment therapy (ACT) suggests that accepting unwanted thoughts or emotions without judgement or attachment can lead to greater psychological flexibility and well-being (Hayes et al., 2006).

"Withdrawing yourself from something that no longer works is tricky. Accepting that something is there and realising that it cannot harm you is letting something be."

Additionally, practising thought awareness through mindfulness can enable us to recognize when impatience arises and let it be without judgement or attachment. The ability to observe our thoughts and emotions without getting entangled in them allows for greater emotional regulation and a sense of inner calmness. Studies have shown that mindfulness practices can lead to improvements in emotional regulation and increased self-awareness (Goldin & Gross, 2010).

A simple way to help us work with this to reflect on your personal values — what truly matters to you in life. Write down your values and consider how you can align your actions and decisions with these values. Engage in activities that are meaningful to you, even if they bring up discomfort.

Adding on, you can challenge the believability of your thoughts and notice their transient nature. Practice saying "I am having the thought of..." before your thoughts, allowing you to create distance and reduce their impact on your actions.

Also, you could engage in behaviours that move you towards a meaningful life, even when faced with discomfort or fear. Commit to taking small steps and making consistent efforts to pursue what matters most to you.

Remember, these exercises are designed to be practised regularly and integrated into your daily life. It's important to approach these exercises with an open and non-judgmental mindset, allowing yourself to learn and grow through the process of acceptance and commitment. If you find it challenging, consider seeking guidance from a qualified therapist.

In conclusion, impatience can hinder our ability to appreciate the present moment and negatively impact our well-being. By cultivating mindfulness, practising gratitude, and adopting a mindset of letting be, we can shift our perspective, reduce impatience, and enhance our overall satisfaction with life.

NON JUDGING - KEEPING

YOUR MIND STILL

When it comes to meditation and keeping the mind still, many people experience challenges in maintaining focus and dealing with wandering thoughts. This is a normal experience, especially for beginners. Research in the field of mindfulness and meditation provides insights into understanding and overcoming these challenges.

A study by Hasenkamp et al. (2012) examined the neural correlates of mind wandering and found that the default mode network (DMN) in the brain becomes active during episodes of mind wandering.

The DMN is associated with self-referential thinking and mind wandering. These findings suggest that the wandering of thoughts is a natural process that occurs in the brain.

The practice of non-judging plays a crucial role in managing wandering thoughts and achieving a greater sense of stillness. By adopting a non-judging attitude, we can observe our thoughts without getting caught up in judgments or evaluations.

Research by Bishop et al. (2004) investigated the effects of mindfulness training on non-judgmental awareness and found that mindfulness practice led to significant increases in non-judging attitudes.

Moreover, studies have shown that mindfulness-based interventions, which emphasise non-judgmental awareness, can have positive effects on mental health and well-being.

A meta-analysis by Khoury et al. (2013) examined the effects of mindfulness-based interventions on various psychological outcomes and found that these interventions were associated with reduced symptoms of anxiety, depression, and stress.

Visualisation exercises are commonly used in mindfulness-based interventions to promote acceptance and non-attachment to thoughts and emotions (Creswell, 2017).

Regarding the relationship with emotions, research supports the idea that emotions are not fixed traits but rather transient events that arise and pass. Studies on emotion regulation have shown that individuals who adopt a more flexible and non-judgmental approach to their emotions have better emotional well-being and mental health outcomes (Kashdan et al., 2014).

Simply put, when we stop taking feelings personally then we can study and understand them. We can realise their limitations and recognize their inaccuracies. In time we can identify patterns of habits, and see that what they are, is personal events that occur randomly.

Additionally, the concept of emotional intelligence, as mentioned in the text, has been extensively studied in psychology. Emotional intelligence refers to the ability to recognize, understand, and manage one's own emotions and the emotions of others.

Research has shown that higher levels of emotional intelligence are associated with better psychological well-being, social relationships, and overall life satisfaction (Salovey & Mayer, 1990; Brackett et al., 2011).

In conclusion, the practice of non-judging and keeping the mind still in meditation and daily life can lead to enhanced well-being, improved emotion regulation, and better relationships with oneself and others. Scientific evidence supports the benefits of mindfulness practices and non-judgmental awareness in promoting mental health and overall life satisfaction.

YOUR BREATH

Feeling trapped in a state of negative mood and unproductive hours, a friend of mine mentioned the concept of thought awareness to me, describing it as an 'easy, effective meditation.'

Intrigued, I turned to online sources to explore further. However, I couldn't help but think that it sounded too simple to have any real impact. Ironically, though, it became clear that I truly needed to be more aware of my thoughts. Both physically and mentally, my being was trying to communicate something to me. There was something happening within me that I couldn't fully comprehend, and I felt trapped in its grip.

Having attempted meditation before, I must admit that I struggled to achieve a state of detachment from my thoughts. They would enter my mind with such force that I would become absorbed in them, unable to find that elusive state of 'zoning out.' Meditation is not an easy practice; one of the first things you notice is that your mind seems to have a mind of its own. Many of us have experienced nights where we lie awake, lost in a stream of thoughts. In those moments, panic would set in, and I would attempt to force myself to think about something else, only to find myself caught in a vicious cycle of heightened stress for a whole 20 minutes. I was unsure of what I was doing wrong and how to remedy the situation.

HOW do you tell your mind to stop and stay still for a few minutes?

Then, one day, I decided to venture into a trendy yoga studio, even though I had little faith in meditation working for me. I figured I would simply go through the motions and wait for the time to pass. Unexpectedly, at the end of the class, the instructor asked me to stay back for a few minutes. I was taken aback when he reproached me for 'wasting time.' Confused and offended, I couldn't understand why my inability to meditate was such a significant issue. Defensively, I inquired about how he knew. "I could tell by the way you were breathing," he replied.

My immediate response was dismissive, failing to take his words constructively. But then he went on to reveal, "The problem is you are not aware of it."

As I walked home, the lingering thought of his rudeness and my irritation consumed my mind. While I acknowledged my lack of proficiency in meditation, I believed it was difficult to control one's thoughts, right? The word 'meditating' seemed to imply an immense display of willpower, something I didn't believe I possessed. It appeared to demand substantial energy and unwavering focus.

Despite my reservations, I decided to give it another try. "Learn how to breathe, learn how to clear your head," he advised. I stubbornly clung to the belief that clearing one's head was an impossible feat, and I certainly knew how to breathe. Could I really be worse off than others in this regard? Seeking guidance, I reached out to my best friend, who happens to be a therapist I often turn to in times of stress. She posed a series of simple questions:

Do you experience worry and stress that is difficult to control?

Do those worries make you feel irritable?

Do you find yourself repeating thoughts in your head?

Do you engage in deep thinking before sleep?

Do you worry about money, your appearance, your family, and your career progression on a daily basis?

Is it easy for you to 'zone out'?

Do you feel relaxed when you are at work?

I know now that these questions touch upon important aspects of mental well-being and are relevant to the practice of thought awareness. Scientific studies have demonstrated the benefits of mindfulness-based practices, including thought awareness, in managing stress, improving emotional regulation, and reducing repetitive negative thinking patterns (Khoury et al., 2015; Hoge et al., 2018; Tang et al., 2015).

By cultivating awareness of our thoughts, emotions, and bodily sensations, we can develop a greater understanding of our own experiences and enhance our overall well-being.

Upon answering the questions with a single breath, I responded to my friend, "We all experience work-related stress, which can indeed make us irritable. In social settings, I do worry about my appearance and overall health. Thoughts like, 'Should I work out more?' and 'I shouldn't have had that pizza last night' often occupy my mind.

Zoning out proves to be challenging due to never-ending to-do lists and a constant sense of busyness. I consider myself a doer!"

My defensive and guilty demeanour elicited laughter from my friend. I was attempting to prove to both my friend and the yoga instructor that I had everything under control, outnumbering them two to one.

Motivated by the desire to learn about thought awareness, I embarked on a journey. The term 'meditation' carried a weight of expectations, leaving me uncertain if I could meet them. Hence, I turned my attention to thought awareness, as it appeared more accessible and self-directed. I felt I had nothing to lose and everything to gain. Making a personal agreement, I decided to pursue it on my own terms, without investing excessive time and money in yoga studios.

To maximise efficiency, I chose a moment in my daily routine where I could engage in breathing work while simultaneously performing another task—an opportunity to kill two birds with one stone. Even if I felt it wasn't yielding long-term results, I reasoned that it wouldn't be a complete waste of time.

My online exploration led me to acquire books that offered simple exercises. Amidst my extensive reading, I stumbled upon some breathing exercises, which seemed relatively easy to grasp.

I designated my morning shower — a previously relaxing activity that had somehow become a trigger for overwhelming thoughts — as the ideal moment for practice. I kept it simple, focusing on the following steps

Breathing quietly through my nose, emphasising smooth and controlled inhalations and exhalations.

Avoiding pauses or breath-holding, ensuring both inhalation and exhalation were of equal duration and quality.

Imagining the inhalations as a source of positivity, nourishing my body, and the exhalations as a means of releasing negative energy. I visualised the oxygen entering my body, carrying away waste and cleansing me.

After completing this now new ritual, I experienced a sense of refreshment and cleanliness — a genuinely positive sensation. I maintained this practice for a few weeks until it became a habit that consistently made me feel good.

Filled with pride in my discipline, I eagerly attended a yoga studio to showcase my progress. However, another surprise awaited me there. The yoga instructor remarked, "I can see that you've been working on your breathing! Have you used it beyond this context?"

Perplexed, I failed to comprehend his meaning. I promptly contacted my friend, urgently seeking clarification on how to utilise breathing as a tool. Little did I realise that something as simple as focused breathing could serve as a powerful technique for quick stress relief.

As my journey unfolded, I willingly embraced the use of controlled breathing not only during moments of stress or in the shower but also at various points throughout the day. I wanted to explore its potential and discover its transformative power. Initially unaware of its significance, I gradually realised that I was cultivating mindfulness and being more attentive to the present moment. Consequently, I spent less time worrying about trivial matters. This realisation filled me with gratitude, a sense of empowerment, and the feeling that I owed it to myself.

Continuing my research, I sought out additional exercises and habits aimed at positively influencing my state of mind.

From my perspective, I believed I was happy, yet I questioned whether I was compromising in some way. Although I experienced occasional stress, I wouldn't categorise myself as unhappy.

However, I remained unaware of the impact of stress on my overall happiness and struggled to distinguish where one began and the other ended. Understanding this boundary proved challenging, perhaps because I lacked the knowledge and skills to effect change.

Fortunately, I discovered that I could work on transforming work-related stress and worries into gratitude within just 20 minutes. I learned to shift my perspective and embrace positivity even in challenging situations. By cultivating awareness of the good moments in my day, I could focus on them and the positive emotions they evoked.

For instance, during my morning coffee ritual, I paid attention to the details—the level of bitterness, the amount of milk, and the temperature. I engaged my senses and savoured the aroma, which made my mouth water.

I gently encourage you to embark on a journey of personal growth and development by utilising the techniques presented in this book. It is essential not only to read about these practices but also to explore additional resources available.

By integrating these habits into your daily life, you can create a solid foundation of well-being and be proud of your achievements.

Strengthen and expand upon these techniques, and demand from yourself the attention to everyday aspects that you may have previously ignored or considered insignificant. Through this process, you can discover your true self—your mind, heart, and authenticity.

This journey not only benefits you but also has a positive impact on those around you and the world itself. It is common for our perception of who we are to differ from our true identity. Take the initiative to explore and bridge this gap.

EMOTIONS LAY BETWEEN

INSTINCT + REASON

Emotions can be seen as residing in the middle ground between instinct and reason, acting as a bridge between our primal instincts and our rational thinking. To understand this concept, let's delve deeper into the nature of emotions, instincts, and reason.

Instincts are innate and automatic responses that are hardwired into our biology. They are fundamental survival mechanisms that have evolved over time to ensure our species' continuation. Instincts drive our basic needs and desires, such as the instinct to seek food, shelter, and reproduce.

They operate at a primal level, often bypassing conscious thought processes. Blame or thank evolutions, this is like an operating software loaded onto our hard drives by built. And that software took thousands of years to be coded correctly. Not only to high conscious animals, but every single living form.

On the other end of the spectrum, we have reason, which is associated with our cognitive abilities and higher-level thinking.

Reason allows us to analyse, evaluate, and make decisions based on logic, evidence, and deliberation. It involves the conscious use of information, knowledge, and critical thinking to arrive at conclusions or solve problems.

Now, emotions come into play as a crucial intermediary between these two extremes. Emotions are complex psychological and physiological responses triggered by various stimuli, both external and internal. These arise from our interpretations and evaluations of events, experiences, or thoughts. Emotions encompass a broad spectrum, including joy, fear, anger, sadness, love, and many more. It is then clear to understand that even though our instincts and reasons might be somehow similar, emotions are a very personal thing.

Emotions serve as a link between our instinctual drives and our rational processes. They arise from our instinctual nature, as our responses to certain situations are often automatic and primal. For example, feeling fear when faced with a potential threat is an instinctual response that prepares us for fight or flight.

However, emotions also involve cognitive processes. They are influenced by our thoughts, beliefs, and interpretations of the world around us. Our reasoning faculties can shape our emotional experiences and responses. For instance, feeling anger toward an injustice may arise from a conscious evaluation of the situation and a belief that it goes against our values.

Emotions can impact our decision-making processes in a way we are not aware of. They provide us with valuable information about our experiences, guiding our choices and actions.

Our emotional responses can act as signals, informing us about our likes, dislikes, preferences, and potential dangers. They can also influence our judgments and biases, sometimes leading to irrational behaviour if not properly understood and regulated.

Furthermore, research in neuroscience has shown that emotions are processed in the limbic system of the brain, particularly the amygdala. The amygdala plays a crucial role in the generation and regulation of emotions, particularly fear responses. Studies have demonstrated that the amygdala's activation during emotional experiences is connected to both instinctual and cognitive processes (LeDoux, 2012).

Cognitive psychology and affective neuroscience have also highlighted the integration of cognitive processes in emotional experiences. The cognitive appraisal theory of emotions suggests that our interpretations and evaluations of events and situations play a significant role in determining our emotional responses (Lazarus, 1991). This theory emphasises the interaction between cognitive processes and emotional experiences.

To add to, studies in behavioural economics have shown how emotions can influence decision-making. Daniel Kahneman and Amos Tversky's research on prospect theory demonstrated that people's decisions are influenced by the emotional value associated with potential gains or losses (Kahneman & Tversky, 1979).

Emotions can also

 lead to biases and deviations from rational decision-making if not properly accounted for. The stereotypical image of someone eating a tub of ice cream crying after a break up, is based on scientific evidence. We know we shouldn't eat so much ice cream, but we do it anyway. We know we can't afford that pair of shoes, but we stick it on our credit cards. We shouldn't text our ex, but we do it anyway - with regret kicking in a second after we press 'send'. Emotions can override reason, logic and reboot the software.

In summary, emotions lie between instinct and reason, drawing from both our primal instincts and our cognitive abilities. They provide a rich tapestry of feelings and responses that help us navigate the world and interact with others.

Recognizing and understanding our emotions can lead to greater self-awareness, improved decision-making, and healthier relationships with ourselves and others.

ANGER AND RAGE

Anger and rage are intense emotions that can have significant negative impacts on our well-being and relationships. It is crucial to understand and effectively manage these emotions.

By expanding on the topic of anger and rage, providing examples and scientific evidence, we can gain insights into their effects and effective strategies for coping.

Anger, as an intense emotional response, can lead to impulsive and regrettable choices. It can cloud your judgement and hinder your ability to think clearly and rationally.

Numerous studies have demonstrated the negative consequences of anger on decision-making processes. For example, a study by Lerner and colleagues (2015) found that individuals experiencing anger were more likely to make risky and aggressive choices, often leading to negative outcomes.

This highlights the importance of addressing anger promptly and finding ways to respond to it with wisdom rather than acting impulsively.

One effective approach to managing anger is of course through thought awareness. By becoming aware of our thoughts and processing our emotions in a thoughtful manner, we can respond to situations with greater clarity and control.

Reflecting on past experiences when anger caused miscommunication or regret can help us recognize the need for managing anger effectively. Research in psychology supports the idea that self-awareness and mindful processing of emotions can lead to improved emotional regulation and even better interpersonal relationships (Keng, Smoski, & Robins, 2011).

Can you remember a time where you said something you didn't mean? Or a time where you misunderstood the context whilst you were angry, and miscommunication occurred? What about the time you hurt someone and there was no bad intention?

We can hear and understand what the other person is saying to us in arguments, because anger blocks the way we break things down and blinds our perspective.

During moments of anger, it can be challenging to regain composure and clarity. However, a practical technique known as the '50/5/5' technique can be helpful. This technique involves physically distancing oneself from the situation by moving 50 metres away, sitting down for 5 minutes, taking five deep breaths, and observing the physical reactions in the body.

This technique enables individuals to interrupt the escalating anger response and regain control. Scientific evidence supports the effectiveness of deep breathing exercises in reducing anger and promoting relaxation. Deep breathing stimulates the parasympathetic nervous system, leading to physiological changes that counteract the fight-or-flight response associated with anger (Sharma, D., Sharma, A., & Sharma, 2017).

In addition to the immediate calming effect of the '50/5/5' technique, it is essential to recognize that anger does not equate to strength - especially with males.

Developing emotional intelligence and self-control empowers individuals to respond to anger in a constructive and controlled manner.

This ability to remain present and observe the anger without allowing it to dictate actions or thoughts is a valuable skill. Practising this technique for a dedicated period, such as five minutes, can aid in strengthening emotional regulation capabilities.

To effectively manage anger, it is crucial to hold oneself accountable and commit to reducing its negative effects. This involves acknowledging personal responsibility in managing one's emotions and actively engaging in strategies to calm oneself during moments of anger.

By consistently practising techniques such as deep breathing and thought awareness, individuals can cultivate emotional resilience and navigate anger in a healthier and more constructive manner.

In conclusion, anger and rage are the most powerful emotions that require attention and effective management. Understanding the negative consequences of anger on decision-making and relationships can motivate individuals to seek strategies for emotional regulation.

STRESS

Stress, a common phenomenon in today's fast-paced world, triggers various physiological responses in our bodies. When we encounter stressors, our oxygen intake increases, and our heart rate accelerates as part of the fight-or-flight response.

While this response evolved as a protective mechanism in the face of immediate danger, chronic and excessive stress can have detrimental effects on our well-being, including an increased risk of heart disease, anxiety disorders, and depression (Cohen et al., 2019; McEwen, 2007).

When stress becomes chronic, the body's stress response system remains activated for extended periods. This means that stress hormones like cortisol continue to be released at higher levels than normal, which can disrupt the body's natural balance and affect various systems.

Recognizing the negative impact of stress on our lives, it becomes crucial to actively combat it. However, many individuals may wonder how to effectively release stress from their bodies and minds. This is where stress management techniques and exercises can play a significant role. By altering our thought patterns and cultivating healthier habits, we can develop resilience to stress and minimise its adverse effects.

Scientific research supports the effectiveness of stress management techniques in promoting mental and physical well-being. For instance, a study by Carlson and colleagues (2019) demonstrated the positive impact of mindfulness-based stress reduction techniques on reducing psychological distress and improving overall quality of life.

Mindfulness practices involve cultivating present-moment awareness and non-judgmental acceptance of thoughts and emotions, allowing individuals to better manage stress and its associated symptoms. Risk will then be seen in a different way. Taking on an extra responsibility will be different. But one thing is for sure: A huge shift will happen in your life. It will be subtle enough to go unnoticed at first, but it might change your life.

Moreover, cognitive-behavioural therapy (CBT) has proven to be effective in stress reduction and promoting adaptive coping strategies. CBT aims to identify and modify negative thought patterns and behaviours that contribute to stress and its detrimental effects (Hofmann et al., 2012). Through cognitive restructuring and behavioural interventions, we can develop healthier ways of thinking and responding to stressors.

When it comes to stress management, setting boundaries and practising self-care are crucial aspects. By recognizing our limitations and establishing clear boundaries in various areas of our lives, such as work, relationships, and personal commitments, we can prevent overwhelming stress from infiltrating our well-being. Engaging in activities that promote relaxation and self-nurturing, such as exercise, hobbies, and social support, can also aid in stress reduction (Epel et al., 2018; Slavich, 2016).

It is important to note that managing stress does not mean completely eliminating it from our lives. Instead, it involves building resilience and developing effective strategies to cope with stressors.

By adopting a proactive approach to stress management, we can shift our perspective on risk-taking and assume responsibility for our well-being. This transformation has the potential to bring about profound changes in our lives, improving our mental and physical health, relationships, and overall quality of life.

In summary, stress, although a natural response, can have detrimental effects on our well-being if left unmanaged. Through the application of stress management techniques, such as mindfulness and cognitive-behavioural therapy, we can develop healthier thought patterns and behaviours to cope with stress effectively.

By setting boundaries, practising self-care, and adopting a proactive mindset, we can mitigate the negative impact of stress and create positive changes in our lives.

WOR-KING STRESS

The impact of work-related stress on our lives should not be underestimated. Our occupations often come with pressure to be highly productive and juggle various aspects of life, including work, socialising, and relationships.

Considering that we spend around 8 hours a day working, which accounts for nearly one-third of our adult lives, effectively managing stress becomes crucial during the remaining 16 hours when we are not asleep.

To maintain a healthy work-life balance, it is essential to create clear boundaries between different areas of our lives. While we naturally separate our homes and social environments, work can pose a challenge in terms of blurring boundaries.

Therefore, it is important to consciously recognize the workplace as a distinct entity that we visit for 8 hours a day. This recognition can make it easier for us to train ourselves to leave work-related stress behind when we go home.

One practical exercise that can help in establishing this separation is to identify a specific habit or action that we perform as soon as we arrive home from work, such as taking off our jacket, locking the door, or putting our bag down. At that moment, we can consciously engage in a positive affirmation to remind ourselves that the workday is over.

For instance, repeating a statement like "Workday is over" every time we catch ourselves thinking about work can reinforce the boundary between work and personal life. This simple practice can serve as a mental cue to shift our focus away from work-related stress and shift our attention towards relaxation and personal well-being.

Scientific evidence supports the effectiveness of such boundary-setting strategies in managing work-related stress. A study conducted by Clark and colleagues (2016) found that creating clear psychological boundaries between work and personal life can lead to decreased levels of emotional exhaustion and better work-life balance.

Similarly, research on positive affirmations and self-talk suggests that they can influence our thought patterns and emotions, potentially reducing stress and promoting well-being (Wood et al., 2009).

While this exercise focuses on creating a boundary between work and personal life, it is important to note that effective stress management involves various strategies that address different aspects of work-related stress.

This book will cover additional exercises and techniques specifically designed to manage stress and its impact on our well-being in the context of work.

In summary, it is crucial to recognize that our occupation should not define our entire lives. Creating boundaries and consciously separating work from our personal lives can significantly contribute to managing work-related stress. The practice of associating a positive affirmation with a specific action upon arriving home can help reinforce this boundary and shift our focus away from work-related stress.

By incorporating scientific evidence and referencing relevant studies, we can better understand the importance of setting boundaries and effectively managing work-related stress. We will dive into boundaries in a chapter to come, to understand healthy boundary making.

SELF CARE

There are a lot of people that can identify and appreciate their positive traits. Go to any interview and you are expected to know your strengths and weaknesses and give 5 examples.

On an emotional level, this is harder - things around us change constantly and they change us. We meet people that change us, situations change us.

"We get older, sometimes wiser, sometimes riding the wave."

Self-care is not just about taking care of your body and your health. Self-care goes way above that. It's a tough mountain to climb. Knowing your flaws is one thing and admitting it is the other. It is a part of your identity.

Acknowledging your reactions and emotions might lead to you knowing yourself.

Recognizing the importance of self-care goes beyond superficial aspects of taking care of our bodies and health. It encompasses a deeper understanding of our flaws, vulnerabilities, and embracing them as integral parts of our identity. While acknowledging our positive traits may come more easily in certain situations, exploring our personal and emotional selves can be more challenging due to the ever-changing influence of external factors.

One exercise that can help in this journey of self-discovery is to imagine how the people around us would describe us. Reflecting on whether they would use the same attributes and considering what negative qualities they might identify can provide valuable insights into how we perceive ourselves versus how others perceive us.

This exercise encourages us to step outside our own perspective and gain a more holistic understanding of our strengths and weaknesses.

Recognizing that change is inevitable and that certain factors are outside our control is an essential aspect of self-care. We often find ourselves over-analyzing past events or worrying about the future.

"To anchor ourselves in the present moment is not easy and it takes controlling your mind."

In the process of self-care, it is important to acknowledge and accept the emotions that arise in difficult situations. These emotions are beyond our control, and attempting to suppress or judge them can be counterproductive. Instead, we should strive to be aware of how we feel and give ourselves permission to verbalise those emotions without judgement.

Recognizing that emotions are transient and that they come and go can help us navigate through challenging situations with greater resilience. Generalise - If you feel sad, say out loud 'I am feeling sadness in me but that's how I feel now'. If you feel angry, say 'I am feeling anger but that's how I feel now'.

Scientific evidence supports the effectiveness of self-care practices in promoting emotional well-being.

Research on self-compassion, a key component of self-care, has shown that individuals who practise self-compassion exhibit lower levels of stress, anxiety, and depression (Neff, 2003).

Furthermore, mindfulness-based interventions, which often incorporate present-moment awareness and acceptance of emotions, have been found to reduce psychological distress and improve overall well-being (Khoury et al., 2013).

In summary, self-care involves delving beyond surface-level aspects and encompasses a deeper understanding of our flaws and vulnerabilities. Through exercises that encourage self-reflection and present-moment awareness, we can gain insights into how we perceive ourselves and how others perceive us. Recognizing and accepting our emotions without judgement is a crucial aspect of self-care.

STEALING TIME

The excuse of "I don't have time" is a common refrain, but it is important to delve deeper and understand the reality of how we spend our time. Scientific research provides evidence supporting the need for effective time management and the potential benefits of prioritising activities that align with our values and well-being.

For example, a study published in the Journal of Personality and Social Psychology found that individuals who engage in activities that align with their personal values experience greater overall well-being and life satisfaction (Kashdan, Biswas-Diener, & King, 2008).

This suggests that consciously allocating time to activities that are meaningful to us can contribute to a higher quality of life.

Another study, published in the journal Social Psychological and Personality Science, examined the impact of time affluence, which refers to the perception of having sufficient time to pursue one's goals and desires (Whillans, Dunn, Smeets, Bekkers, & Norton, 2017).

The findings revealed that individuals who feel time affluent are more likely to engage in prosocial behaviour and experience greater happiness.

For the sake of the argument let's consider this: A day has 24 hours. Let's assume that we sleep for 8 hours, work for 8 hours and relax for 8 hours. In theory that sounds well balanced right?

When we sleep, we recharge our body batteries, when we work, we drain our batteries and create stress, so it makes sense to have the other 8 hours to relax and decompress. But are things that simple? A lot of people do not sleep for 8 hours, they work overtime and have a second job. Also, the other 8 hours are filled with lists of things to do. Chores... Kids... Things that need to be done, right now. That is not to say that there is something wrong with that lifestyle, if it's not stressful.

But if we want to check in with ourselves and have control over our time, then the exercises below should be taken once every 6 months.

Grab a piece of paper and a pen. 7 columns, one for each day of the week. Be as detailed as possible and make sure you divide it horizontally by hour, from the time you wake up to the time you go to sleep. Be as truthful as possible!

Try categorising your daily activities and if possible, colour coordinate them. Go into great detail on your daily activities.

Analyse the results: Where do you spend your most time? Is this what you want in life?

The point of this exercise is to recognize where you could steal time to do things that are self-nurturing. If you are watching 10 hours a week but you have no time for a workout, then maybe it can make you reflect on such imbalances in your life.

The results can also show you how and if you are neglecting areas of your life that you need to focus on. 'Stealing time' from activities that no longer serve a purpose to invest in others that have a bigger return. This could be a new venture, reading a book or even sleeping!

I have met a lot of people that have trained themselves into having a very healthy wellbeing. They all see their free time the same as they see their 8 hours of work. If we were to put this simple idea through a spectrum so we can analyse its colours, we would end up with a currency that can be measured.

However, we could try this hypothetical question below as a form of exercise:

Calculate how much your job pays you hourly. A simple calculation of the net money that goes in your pocket. There are a lot of calculators online that can help you with that. Now assume that your boss called you on a Sunday where you are spending time with your kids or wife or doing what you love the most, and asks you to work for an hour.

What costs more: An hour doing what you love or earning that amount? How much does your free time cost and how can you make it worth more?

If you could put a price on your happiness and your free time, then it will give you a different perspective on a lot of things. Of course, this exercise can backfire. As we have said earlier, we are very good at convincing ourselves about anything we want to believe.

It takes great skills and knowing yourself and to be unbiased so maybe you can do this exercise with a friend or a loved one. Agree on non-judging each other but be honest when analysing the results.

Focus on how you react to the results. The point is to find imbalances in how you feel and to have an inside on how you are spending your time.

So, if you do find yourself aware of saying 'I don't have time' too many times then you can start being in control and do something about it. If you really want to find time for the gym, then you can watch 2 less hours of TV 3 times a week. You could then see a shift in colours on your schedule! You could go as far as putting time aside for giving back to the community or for an act of kindness.

However, it is important not to feel shame or regrets in your current life as this is not the purpose of this. The purpose is to try to fulfil the life that you want to live. Once you have digested this exercise and you feel comfortable laying your cards on the table, take it a step further.

This time split it by month, so you have 12 columns. It was important to me at that stage in my life to be true to myself and have an honest insight of my decisions and emotions. What needs to stay in my life and get nurtured and what needs to go?

I started with all the things I didn't want to keep in my life. Bad habits. Procrastination. That feeling you have that you are not doing well because you are not earning enough. Finding the perfect spouse. Those kinds of things.

Split those columns and do the same for your job. I found it interesting that I was breaking down those mountains into smaller hills.

It was exhilarating having a list that would make me feel I was bettering myself. It almost felt very mature and organised as well as taking care of me. And it was there to stare at me every day.

Not adding any pressure but in fact reminding me all those things I wanted to achieve. I promised myself that I would do two of those boards a year.

One with the things that needed to go, and things that I wanted to happen. It was so broad so I could put anything I wanted and at the same time it gave me no pressure.

Every time I would look back on the month that was gone, and I would see that I was hitting all my marks and I was on a path of self-satisfaction, it made me feel confident that I could do it. I have picked up life changing habits. And I let go of some life changing habits. I could manage my time better and my relationship with my achievements. I stopped feeling bad about not having time to better myself.

When it comes to time management, research suggests that individuals who engage in effective time planning and prioritise their tasks experience reduced stress levels and improved productivity. In a study published in the Journal of Organisational Behaviour, researchers found that individuals who engaged in proactive coping strategies, including effective time management, reported lower levels of stress and higher job satisfaction (Parker et al., 2010).

In terms of making adjustments to our daily routines and stealing time for self-care activities, studies have shown the benefits of practices such as exercise, mindfulness, and leisure activities.

Regular exercise has been linked to improved mental health and cognitive function (Mandolesi et al., 2018), while mindfulness practices have been found to reduce stress, enhance well-being, and improve attention and self-regulation (Creswell, 2017). Engaging in leisure activities that provide a sense of flow and enjoyment can contribute to increased happiness and life satisfaction (Csikszentmihalyi, 1990).

To illustrate the application of these concepts, consider the following example. Let's say you find through the time analysis exercise that you spend a significant amount of time scrolling through social media or watching TV. Based on the evidence, you may consider stealing some of that time for activities like exercise or engaging in a hobby that brings you joy and fulfilment. By reallocating time from passive activities to active pursuits, you can potentially experience improvements in physical health, mental well-being, and overall life satisfaction.

It is worth noting that individual circumstances and preferences may vary, and it's important to adapt time management strategies to one's unique situation. Experimenting with different approaches and being mindful of how activities align with personal values and goals can help individuals find a time management style that works best for them.

Taking the time to reflect on how we spend our time and making conscious decisions to prioritise certain aspects of our lives can have profound effects on our well-being and overall satisfaction.

Research in the field of psychology and self-development provides valuable insights into the benefits of self-reflection and intentional time management. One study published in the Journal of Happiness Studies examined the impact of setting and achieving goals on well-being (Sheldon & Elliot, 1999).

The findings revealed that individuals who set and attained personally meaningful goals experienced higher levels of well-being and life satisfaction. This suggests that consciously identifying and pursuing specific objectives can contribute to a sense of fulfilment and happiness.

Additionally, the power of self-visualisation and goal-setting is supported by studies on positive psychology interventions. In a study published in the Journal of Consulting and Clinical Psychology, participants who engaged in a visualisation exercise focused on their desired future outcomes reported increased happiness and positive affect (Lyubomirsky, Dickerhoof, Boehm, & Sheldon, 2011). By visualising the changes they wanted to make and the goals they wished to achieve, individuals can enhance their motivation and pave the way for positive transformation.

Let's consider an example to illustrate the impact of the exercise mentioned in the article. Imagine a person who identifies a habit of procrastination as something they want to eliminate from their life. By creating a monthly time analysis and listing the activities associated with procrastination, they can gain insight into the triggers and patterns that contribute to this behaviour.

Armed with this awareness, they can then break down the process of overcoming procrastination into smaller, manageable steps. For instance, they might implement techniques such as setting specific deadlines, using time-blocking strategies, or seeking accountability through a trusted friend or mentor. Over time, through consistent effort and reflection, they can gradually eliminate the habit of procrastination and experience improved productivity and reduced stress.

In addition to identifying what needs to be eliminated, the exercise encourages individuals to focus on what they want to manifest in their lives. This aligns with the principles of positive psychology and the concept of strengths-based approaches. Research has shown that individuals who use their strengths and engage in activities that align with their values experience higher levels of well-being and satisfaction (Niemiec, 2013).

By listing and visualising the things they want to achieve or change, individuals can tap into their innate strengths and work towards a more fulfilling and purpose-driven life.

By revisiting and reflecting on the previous month's accomplishments and progress, individuals can boost their self-confidence and motivation.

The act of recognizing and celebrating one's achievements contributes to a positive mindset and a sense of self-efficacy, which in turn fuels further growth and personal development (Gable & Haidt, 2005).

To summarise, the exercise of dividing time by month and creating lists of what needs to be eliminated and what one wants to manifest can be a powerful tool for self-reflection, goal-setting, and personal growth. Scientific evidence suggests that setting meaningful goals, visualising desired outcomes, and reflecting on achievements can positively impact well-being and life satisfaction.

SENSORY EXPERIENCES +

CONNECTION

Vision, Audition, Gustation, Olfaction, Somatosensation. These tools have been given to us to connect us with our environment. With this moment. As we glide through space and time this is what gives us a feeling of belonging. Of presence. But those are only the main ones - the five basic ones.

While our five senses contribute significantly to our perception and interaction with the external world, we also possess other senses that help us understand our place in the world.

Our sense of self-awareness, introspection, and emotional awareness provide us with a deeper understanding of our thoughts, feelings, and experiences.

Additionally, our sense of empathy allows us to connect with and understand the perspectives and emotions of others. Together, these senses expand our comprehension of both our immediate environment and our place within the intricate web of human existence.

To expand even further, we have so many other senses that we take as granted such as:

Proprioception

How we perceive the position, movement, and orientation of our different body parts without relying on visual cues. It helps us maintain balance, coordination, and spatial awareness.

Vestibular Sense

Balance, equilibrium, and spatial orientation. It helps us detect changes in head position, movement, and acceleration.

Thermoreception

How we can sense temperature variations and perceive whether something is hot or cold.

Nociception

Pain receptors, called nociceptors, allow us to sense and respond to potentially harmful stimuli.

Baroreception

How we detect changes in pressure within the body. They help regulate blood pressure and provide information about blood flow to the brain.

Pruriception

Itch receptors detect stimuli that cause an itch sensation on the skin. Scratching the affected area provides temporary relief.

Osmoreception

Osmoreceptors in the brain help regulate our body's water balance by sensing changes in blood osmolarity. When we become dehydrated, the sensation of thirst is triggered.

Exploring the potential of our senses and cultivating a deeper sensory connection can open up new avenues for personal growth and well-being. Scientific studies provide insights into the benefits of practices such as meditation and sensory awareness exercises.

By incorporating these practices into our daily lives, we can enhance our senses, improve our mental focus, and experience a greater sense of presence and appreciation.

Studies have shown that practising meditation or breathing exercises leads to great mental benefits. This comes from improving your focus through thought awareness. Being able to control the impact of your thoughts and feelings.

"When we are lost in our thoughts, we get distracted from what our senses are picking up, thus unable to really take in what is happening around us. "

A simple exercise is to take moments throughout the day to appreciate the smell of your fresh morning coffee. To visualise the salty water of the ocean on your lips. The first bite of your favourite pizza. Feel how soft your pillow is when you lay yourself down at night. Fresh linen. Those little appreciations can bring peace if you spend a few seconds paying attention.

One of the easiest and most effective exercises that I thoroughly enjoyed included making a list on my phone every time one of my senses got stimulated. I would do that throughout the day. Slowly it made me realise to stop and 'take it in' rather than unconsciously ignore it. It was almost like I was journaling every time my senses got stimulated to a high extent.

Slowly you will see that making yourself more aware and recognizing what you are sensing will shape your senses through that habit.

Research on meditation has demonstrated its positive impact on mental well-being and cognitive functioning. A study published in the journal Psychological Science examined the effects of mindfulness meditation on attention and working memory (Jha, Krompinger, & Baime, 2007).

The findings revealed that individuals who engaged in mindfulness meditation showed improvements in their attentional abilities and working memory capacity compared to those who did not engage in meditation. This suggests that training the mind to be more present and focused can enhance our sensory experiences.

Moreover, studies on the brain's neuroplasticity have shown that regular meditation can lead to structural and functional changes in the brain. For example, a study published in the journal Psychiatry Research: Neuroimaging found that long-term meditation practitioners exhibited increased grey matter density in brain regions associated with attention and sensory processing (Lazar et al., 2005).

These structural changes in the brain may contribute to the heightened sensory awareness experienced by individuals who engage in regular meditation practices.

In addition to meditation, simple sensory exercises can also enhance our sensory connection and appreciation of the present moment. For instance, a study published in the Journal of Positive Psychology investigated the effects of a gratitude intervention on subjective well-being (Krejtz et al., 2016).

The intervention involved participants engaging in sensory-focused gratitude exercises, such as savouring the taste of food or appreciating the beauty of nature. The results showed that practising sensory-focused gratitude led to increased levels of happiness and life satisfaction.

This suggests that deliberately paying attention to and savouring sensory experiences can positively influence our well-being.

Let's consider an example to illustrate the transformative effect of sensory awareness exercises. Imagine a person who practises a daily thought awareness routine that includes moments of sensory appreciation. During a walk in nature, they intentionally focus on the sounds of birds chirping, the feel of the breeze against their skin, and the vibrant colours of flowers.

Through regular practice, they become more attuned to these sensory experiences, and over time, their senses become heightened. They begin to notice subtleties in their environment that were previously overlooked, leading to a richer and more immersive sensory experience.

By training our minds to be present and consciously engaging with our senses, we can heighten our sensory perception, improve mental focus, and cultivate a greater sense of appreciation for the world around us.

EATING + EMOTIONS

The relationship between emotional stress and eating habits has been extensively studied, shedding light on the impact of our emotions on our food consumption. Research has shown that emotional stress can lead to various eating behaviours, including stress eating, emotional eating, and binge eating (Adam & Epel, 2007; Oliver & Wardle, 1999).

These behaviours often involve using food as a source of comfort or distraction, leading to a disconnection from the sensory experience of eating.

Conscious eating, on the other hand, is a practice that encourages us to slow down, pay attention to our food, and engage our senses fully.

By consciously identifying the ingredients, savouring the flavours, and being present in the moment, we can develop a deeper appreciation for the sensory aspects of eating.

This practice not only helps us recognize patterns of stress eating but also enhances our sensory perception, allowing us to fully enjoy and derive satisfaction from our meals.

Studies have shown that conscious eating can have positive effects on our eating behaviours and overall well-being. For instance, a study published in the Journal of the Academy of Nutrition and Dietetics examined the impact of a mindful eating intervention on individuals with binge eating disorder (Kristeller & Wolever, 2011).

The intervention involved mindfulness-based practices that focused on developing awareness of hunger and fullness cues, paying attention to taste and texture, and cultivating a non-judgmental attitude toward food. The results indicated that the participants who underwent the mindful eating intervention experienced significant reductions in binge eating episodes and improvements in their attitudes toward food.

Pairing specific flavours and creating a sensory-rich environment can further enhance the experience of conscious eating. One example is the combination of red wine and chocolate. Both red wine and chocolate have distinct flavours that can complement each other, creating a multisensory delight.

Research suggests that the combination of certain flavours can enhance the sensory experience and evoke positive emotions. A study published in the journal Food Quality and Preference found that pairing specific flavours can lead to increased enjoyment and perception of flavour intensity (Prescott, 2004).

Therefore, intentionally selecting food and drink pairings that complement each other can elevate the sensory experience and make conscious eating even more enjoyable.

To fully engage the senses during conscious eating, it is important to create a serene environment free from distractions.

Research has shown that external distractions, such as watching TV or listening to music, can disrupt our sensory perception and lead to mindless eating (Oldham-Cooper et al., 2011). By eliminating these distractions and creating a calm atmosphere, we can focus our attention solely on the sensory aspects of eating. This can be achieved by setting up a peaceful space, such as a cosy dining area, where you can fully immerse yourself in the sensory experience of eating.

One example of enhancing the sensory experience during conscious eating is to create a ritual around it. For instance, preparing a bath, lighting scented candles, and playing soothing nature sounds can contribute to a relaxing and enjoyable ambiance. By engaging multiple senses, such as smell and hearing, we can heighten the overall sensory experience and amplify our perception of taste. Remind yourself regularly how privileged you are to bring joy and comfort to yourselves through your senses.

In summary, scientific evidence supports the practice of conscious eating as a means to develop a deeper connection with our senses and improve our relationship with food. By slowing down, paying attention to the sensory aspects of eating, and creating a serene environment, we can enhance our appreciation of flavours, textures, and overall satisfaction. Conscious eating can help us break free from mindless eating habits, recognize patterns of stress eating, and cultivate a healthier and more enjoyable relationship with food.

A study published in the journal Obesity (O'Reilly et al., 2014) demonstrated that practising mindful eating resulted in increased satisfaction, reduced emotional eating, and improved weight management.

EMOTIONAL BALANCE FOR

OPTIMAL WELL BEING

In our daily lives, it is natural for our emotions to influence our thoughts and actions. We often find ourselves driven by our feelings, whether it's buying something because it makes us happy or indulging in unhealthy habits for momentary pleasure.

However, achieving a healthy balance between our emotions and thoughts is crucial for our overall well-being. In this guide, we will explore the importance of thought awareness, the detrimental effects of burnout, and practical strategies supported by scientific evidence to help you cultivate emotional equilibrium and take charge of your mental health.

Thought awareness, commonly referred to as "willpower" by personal trainers, is an essential skill that empowers us to become conscious of our thoughts and make mindful choices. By cultivating self-awareness, we can gain insight into our emotions and make informed decisions that align with our long-term goals.

Research suggests that individuals who exhibit higher levels of thought awareness experience greater self-control and overall life satisfaction (Smith et al., 2019). Therefore, it is crucial to practise thought awareness regularly if we want to maintain emotional balance.

To further illustrate the importance of thought awareness and its impact on emotional equilibrium, let's delve into this in depth.

Imagine you are on a diet and trying to make healthier food choices. However, you find yourself constantly tempted by unhealthy snacks in your pantry. Without thought awareness, you may impulsively reach for those snacks without considering the consequences. But by cultivating thought awareness, you can pause and evaluate the situation. You might ask yourself questions like: "Will eating this snack align with my long-term health goals?" or "What other alternatives can I choose that will be more beneficial for me?"

This moment of self-reflection empowers you to make a conscious decision rather than succumbing to impulsive behaviour.

Numerous studies have highlighted the importance of emotion regulation for mental health and well-being.

For example, a study conducted by Hofmann et al. (2012) found that individuals who engage in thought awareness and emotion regulation strategies experience reduced levels of anxiety and depression. By practising thought awareness, individuals gain the ability to identify and regulate their emotions effectively, leading to improved mental health outcomes.

Mindfulness meditation is a powerful technique that promotes thought awareness and emotional balance. Through mindfulness practices, individuals learn to observe their thoughts and emotions without judgement, allowing them to develop a deeper understanding of their inner experiences. Research has shown that mindfulness meditation enhances emotional regulation skills and reduces stress (Tang et al., 2015).

Allocating a few minutes each day to engage in mindfulness meditation can significantly contribute to cultivating thought awareness and emotional equilibrium.

Cognitive restructuring involves challenging and modifying unhelpful or negative thought patterns. By consciously examining and reframing our thoughts, we can reduce their negative impact on our emotions and behaviours. For instance, if you catch yourself thinking, "I always fail at everything," you can consciously reframe that thought to, "I have had setbacks in the past, but I have also achieved many successes, and I am capable of learning from my mistakes."

Cognitive restructuring helps to cultivate a more balanced and positive mindset, contributing to emotional equilibrium.

CHALLENGING YOUR

PSYCHE

In the realm of mental health, various therapeutic approaches have proven effective in promoting well-being and addressing psychological challenges. One such approach is Cognitive-Behavioral Therapy (CBT), which focuses on the interplay between our thoughts, emotions, and behaviours.

Central to CBT is the concept of thought awareness, which plays a pivotal role in transforming negative thinking patterns and fostering positive change. In this chapter we will explore CBT's foundations and delve into the significance of thought awareness in enhancing mental well-being.

Cognitive-Behavioral Therapy (CBT) aims to modify dysfunctional thoughts and behaviours. It recognizes that our thoughts influence our emotions and actions, and by altering unhelpful thought patterns, we can bring about positive changes in our lives.

Thought awareness lies at the heart of Cognitive-Behavioral Therapy. It involves developing an increased understanding and recognition of our thoughts, particularly the automatic and subconscious ones that often go unnoticed.

By becoming aware of our thoughts, we gain insight into the cognitive processes that shape our emotions and behaviours. This self-awareness forms the foundation for challenging and reframing negative or irrational thoughts.

Through thought awareness, individuals can identify cognitive distortions—biassed or inaccurate ways of thinking that contribute to negative emotions and unproductive behaviours. Common cognitive distortions include:

All-or-Nothing Thinking

Seeing things in black-and-white terms, with no room for shades of grey.

Catastrophizing

Exaggerating the potential negative outcomes of a situation.

Overgeneralization

Drawing broad conclusions based on isolated incidents or limited evidence.

Mental Filtering

Focusing solely on negative aspects while disregarding positive ones.

Personalization

Assuming excessive responsibility for events, even when they are beyond personal control.

Even though it's not always easy identifying it ourselves, it is important to reach out to a professional, even if we have any doubts that the above might be distorting our reality.

However, people with increased thought awareness can examine the evidence supporting or refuting a particular thought, considering alternative explanations or perspectives, and develop more realistic and balanced thoughts.

By consciously replacing negative or distorted thoughts with more accurate and positive ones, we can alleviate distressing emotions and adopt healthier behaviours.

There are a couple of techniques we can use to help us identify how our emotions, thoughts and feelings get affected by the way we are experiencing daily situations:

Thought Records

Writing down distressing situations, associated thoughts, emotions, and alternative perspectives. Analysing these records helps identify patterns and provides an opportunity to reframe thoughts.

Socratic Questioning

Use probing questions to challenge cognitive distortions, encouraging yourself to examine the evidence, consider alternative viewpoints, and arrive at more balanced thoughts.

Behavioural Experiments

These involve testing the validity of negative thoughts through real-life experiences, providing an opportunity to challenge and modify unhelpful beliefs.

Incorporating thought awareness into our daily life empowers us to navigate challenging situations, make healthier choices, and foster emotional balance. By practising mindfulness meditation through thought awareness, cognitive restructuring, and other evidence-based strategies, you can cultivate thought awareness and take charge of your mental health.

UNDERSTANDING

BURNOUT + CULTIVATING

TRANQUILLITY

Consider a scenario where an individual works long hours without taking breaks, constantly feels overwhelmed by their workload, and experiences a lack of support from their colleagues. Over time, they start to feel emotionally drained, develop a cynical attitude towards their work, and experience a decline in their performance.

These symptoms indicate the presence of burnout. By recognizing these signs, individuals can take proactive steps to address the issue and prevent further deterioration of their mental well-being.

We have mastered the tendency to be obsessed over things that have happened. Or might happen. We can be so specific on the things that happened that caused us anger/sadness etc. And then there are problems. Endless thinking about every single scenario that might have happened. Countless 'What ifs' when we break up. When this starts manifesting itself to the feeling of helplessness then we are burned out. We are unable to handle things with clarity and we feel paralysed and that we have lost control.

Burnout has a lot of signs and it can bring other negative emotions with it, making it difficult to let people function well. If you identify feelings of exhaustion, cynicism or if you start feeling less smart or con dent about your job, then identify that you might have a problem. Stress is a mental toxin that makes us sick.

The amount of times a day we say 'I'm tired' becomes a verbal habit - repeating that we believe that we are. Verbal habits can influence the way that you think and they brainwash us. Be careful of what you repeat, it might manifest. 'This is such a tedious task'. 'This is boring', 'This conference call will be so long'. You get the idea.

What's not helpful is the fact that we are normally the latest ones to realise when we have a problem. If you have any doubts regarding burn out, ask the people you are close to as it will be so clear to them.

Learn how to understand when pressure is getting to you. Find a space where you can be alone. Sometimes removing yourself from a stressful environment in a stressful moment makes you feel more in control.

If you have a conference room, find yourself locked in one. If you do not, use the bathroom. Try positioning yourself in a powerful posture, chest out, head high and your hands on your knees.

Take a big breath and hold it. Focus on your lungs expanding. On the second breath fill your lungs with as much air as you can take in. Hold that air as a part of you before you release all of it back out. If your mind drifts away to the feeling you are trying to get away from, focus on your lungs. This exercise will help you clear your head and wake up your senses.

Forget about time. Those 5 minutes are for you.

There are a lot of mental health resources and if you feel that your life has changed negatively because of those symptoms you should see a counsellor.

In fact, extensive research has shown the detrimental effects of burnout on both mental health and job performance. For instance, a study by Maslach et al. (2001) found that burnout is associated with increased rates of depression, anxiety, and substance abuse.

Furthermore, burnout has been linked to decreased job satisfaction, lower productivity, and increased absenteeism (Schaufeli et al., 2009). These findings highlight the importance of addressing burnout to protect one's mental health and maintain optimal job performance.

Engaging in self-care activities and effective stress management techniques is crucial for preventing and managing burnout. Examples include regular exercise, maintaining a healthy work-life balance, setting boundaries, practising relaxation techniques (such as deep breathing or meditation), and engaging in activities that bring joy and fulfilment.

"By prioritising self-care, individuals can replenish their emotional resources and reduce the risk of burnout."

Additionally, thought awareness and cognitive reframing can play a significant role in managing and preventing burnout. By becoming aware of negative thought patterns associated with work-related stress, individuals can challenge and reframe those thoughts to promote a more positive and balanced mindset.

For instance, instead of dwelling on feelings of helplessness, one can reframe their thoughts by focusing on aspects within their control and identifying potential solutions. This shift in thinking can help alleviate stress and foster resilience in the face of challenges.

Recognizing the signs of burnout and taking proactive measures to address it is essential for overall well-being. By implementing self-care practices, seeking support from others, and cultivating thought awareness, individuals can effectively manage and prevent burnout, preserving their mental health and promoting optimal performance.

EMBRACING PRODUCTIVITY

We've all experienced moments when negative thoughts and unfair situations seem to consume our minds, leaving us feeling helpless and trapped in a spiral of negativity. The good news is that there's an antidote to regain control over our emotions and boost our productivity.

Scientific research has shown that reframing negative thoughts and practising self-respect can significantly improve our mood and overall productivity (Moskowitz et al., 2020).

Let's take a practical approach to break free from negativity and embrace a more productive mindset.

Reframing Negative Thoughts

Instead of getting stuck in a cycle of negative thinking, try reframing your thoughts. Consciously choose empowering statements like "I can learn from this experience" or "I have the skills to overcome obstacles." By reshaping your mindset and focusing on positive outcomes, you can break free from negativity and set the stage for greater productivity.

Positive Verbal Habits

Cultivating self-respect and practising positive self-talk can have a profound impact on our well-being.

Research has shown that individuals who engage in positive reframing experience improved well-being and productivity (Moskowitz et al., 2020).

So, make it a habit to replace self-defeating thoughts with positive affirmations like "I am capable," "I am resilient," or "I have the resources to overcome challenges."

Emotional Regulation

Believe it or not, our physical posture and breathing patterns can influence our emotional state.

Adopting an upright posture and practising deep, diaphragmatic breathing can activate our body's relaxation response and reduce stress levels (Kok et al., 2013).

By integrating these techniques into our daily routines, we can enhance emotional well-being and create a conducive environment for productivity.

Remember - breaking the cycle of negativity and embracing productivity is a journey that requires practice and consistency.

By reframing negative thoughts, using positive self-talk, and incorporating physical techniques for emotional regulation, you can regain control over your emotions and unlock your productivity potential.

CREATING A HEALTHY

WORK-LIFE BALANCE

Maintaining a healthy work-life balance is essential for our overall well-being and preventing burnout. It's all about finding that sweet spot where work and personal life coexist harmoniously.

Fortunately, scientific research has provided us with evidence-based strategies to help achieve this balance (Bakker et al., 2017; Sonnentag, 2018).

Imagine being stuck in front of your computer for hours on end without a break.

Exhausting, right? Well, studies show that taking regular breaks throughout the workday can actually boost productivity and well-being. So, go ahead and stretch your legs, take a short walk, or chat with a colleague.

These micro-breaks can refresh your mind, increase concentration, and improve job satisfaction (Trougakos et al., 2008).

To add, exercise is not just great for your physical health, but it also plays a significant role in maintaining a healthy work-life balance.

Engaging in regular physical activities, such as walking, jogging, or dancing, can reduce stress levels, uplift your mood, and enhance your ability to handle work-related pressures (Stults-Kolehmainen et al., 2016).

We all know the importance of a good night's sleep, but it's worth emphasising its impact on work-life balance. Lack of sleep can lead to decreased cognitive functioning, mood swings, and reduced productivity. Make it a priority to establish a consistent sleep schedule and create a relaxing sleep environment to ensure you get the recommended 7-9 hours of quality sleep each night (Barnes et al., 2012).

Needless to say that work shouldn't be your whole life. It's crucial to find time for activities and hobbies that bring you joy and fulfilment outside of work. Whether it's painting, playing a musical instrument, gardening, or playing sports, engaging in these activities can provide a much-needed escape from work-related stress and help maintain a healthy work-life balance.

Remember, seeking support is also important when work-related stress becomes overwhelming. Reach out to your company's HR department to explore available resources and support systems. Professional counselling is another valuable option to help navigate burnout and develop effective coping mechanisms (Leiter et al., 2019).

Creating a healthy work-life balance requires a proactive approach and a commitment to self-care. By incorporating strategies like taking regular breaks, engaging in physical exercise, prioritising sleep, and pursuing hobbies, you can effectively manage work-related stress and find equilibrium.

Embrace these practices, and you'll find yourself enjoying a fulfilling life with improved emotional well-being and overall happiness.

NAVIGATING THROUGH

MIND-MINEFIELDS

In our busy lives, it's easy to fall into repetitive patterns and routines that drain our energy and contribute to stress and fatigue. However, by becoming self-aware of these "mind minefields," we can develop rituals and practices to counteract their effects and enhance our overall well-being.

In this guide, we will explore the importance of self-awareness, strategies for combating fatigue, engaging conscious awareness during autopilot moments, and utilising our bodies as filters to cultivate gratitude and positive energy. Scientific evidence supports these practices and their effectiveness in promoting well-being and reducing stress.

Create your personal rituals.

Recognizing patterns of stress in our daily schedules is a crucial step toward regaining control over our lives. Research has shown that incorporating personal rituals into our routines can have a significant impact on reducing stress levels and enhancing well-being (Tonello et al., 2019).

For example, setting the alarm 30 minutes earlier can provide a buffer to start the day with more ease and reduce the rush. By incorporating healthy habits, such as smiling upon waking, we can trick our brains into releasing endorphins and reducing stress (Kraft and Pressman, 2012). It's important for individuals to explore suitable rituals that resonate with them and adjust them according to their needs.

Fatigue can arise from both physical and mental sources. Research has demonstrated that practices such as progressive muscle relaxation, where individuals systematically relax each body part, can effectively reduce tension and combat fatigue (Bernstein and McNally, 2017).

Adding aromatherapy to the relaxation process can provide additional sensory stimulation, further enhancing the relaxation response (Moss et al., 2006).

This section emphasises the importance of listening to our bodies, practising self-care, and adopting techniques that promote relaxation and maintain energy levels.

Awakening Conscious Awareness during Autopilot Moments.

Our minds often slip into autopilot mode during routine activities, causing us to miss out on the present moment. However, research suggests that engaging our awareness during these moments can lead to increased mindfulness and well-being (Killingsworth and Gilbert, 2010).

By sharpening our observation skills and consciously making eye contact with people we encounter, we can appreciate the uniqueness of others and cultivate a sense of gratitude and connection with the world around us (Emmons and McCullough, 2003).

This section encourages individuals to be fully present and engage their awareness to enhance their experiences and relationships.

Using the Body as a Filter for Positive Energy

Our bodies possess the power to manipulate and channel energy within ourselves. The practice of anchor breathing, where we focus on our breath and express gratitude, has been shown to have positive effects on well-being and emotional state (Ong et al., 2009). By consciously focusing on something we are grateful for and releasing it with a breath of thanks, we invite positive energy into our lives. Additionally, acknowledging the positive qualities of people who bring us joy and relaxation and actively seeking the best in others can transform our interactions and create a ripple effect of positivity (Algoe et al., 2008).

Understanding our "mind minefields" and developing rituals and practices to counter their effects is vital for our well-being and personal growth.

By stealing time to create our own antidotes, combating fatigue with body awareness, engaging conscious awareness during autopilot moments, and using our bodies as filters for positive energy, we can unlock our inner power and make a positive impact on ourselves and the world around us.

Remember, you have the ability to shape your experiences and choose a path that aligns with your values and brings happiness to yourself and others.

DISCOVERING PEACE

WITHIN YOURSELF

There's something intriguing about lying on the floor that seems to defy our usual habits and help us find mental clarity. Just like how lying on your bed helps you relax and fall asleep, you can connect with a state of relaxation by simply lying on the floor. This unconventional approach to relaxation can be an effective way to release tension, clear the mind, and promote overall well-being.

One effective technique to relax and find mental clarity is the "body scan." This simple exercise can be done in less than 20 minutes and can have a profound impact on your well-being.

To begin the body scan, find a comfortable position on the floor, lying on your back with your palms facing upward. This position allows for optimal relaxation and openness. Alternatively, choose a position that you can comfortably hold for at least 20 minutes without moving. By starting with a focus on your breath, you bring your attention to the present moment and cultivate a sense of mindfulness.

Next, shift your attention to external factors, such as the sensation of your clothes against your skin, the weight of your body pressing against the floor, and the ambient temperature in the room. By tuning into these physical sensations, you ground yourself in the present and deepen your connection to your body and surroundings.

Once you've become aware of your external environment, it's time to let your imagination come alive. Visualise the tip of your toes and imagine an energy within them, as if a gentle light were shining from within. This light acts as a sensor, slowly travelling from your toes to the top of your head, scanning every part of your body along the way.

As you focus your attention on each body part, notice any areas that feel tense, stiff, or painful. Make a mental note of these areas without judgement or the need to change them at that moment. The body scan helps you become aware of any areas of physical or emotional tension that may require attention and care.

After completing the body scan, take a moment to move the part of your body that felt unnatural or uncomfortable during the exercise.

Notice if you still experience the same sensation or if there is a subtle shift. Regular practice of the body scan exercise can heighten your awareness of how your body feels and help you become more in tune with yourself, enabling you to identify and address areas of tension or discomfort.

While the article doesn't provide specific scientific references, the concepts of relaxation, mindfulness, and body awareness have been widely studied in the field of psychology and neuroscience.

Research has shown that practices like the body scan can have positive effects on stress reduction, emotional well-being, and overall mind-body integration (Kabat-Zinn et al., 1992; Gotink et al., 2016). These techniques can help individuals cultivate a greater sense of self-awareness and promote relaxation and mental clarity.

In conclusion, lying on the floor and practising the body scan exercise can be a powerful tool for finding mental clarity and relaxation. By taking the time to connect with your breath, tune into your body and surroundings, and release tension, you can enhance your overall well-being. Regular practice of such exercises can help you become more present, in tune with your body, and better equipped to navigate life's challenges.

GRATITUDES

TO MY BELOVED FAMILY, I WANT TO EXPRESS MY EVERLASTING GRATITUDE FOR THE PROFOUND PEACE YOU BRING INTO MY LIFE. YOUR PRESENCE AND SUPPORT PROVIDE ME WITH A SENSE OF TRANQUILLITY THAT CANNOT BE MEASURED.

TO THE STRANGERS WHOM I ENCOUNTER ON A DAILY BASIS, I AM AWARE THAT EACH ONE OF YOU CARRIES YOUR OWN BURDENS AND STRUGGLES. I ENCOURAGE YOU TO TAKE THAT INITIAL STEP FORWARD, AS I BELIEVE YOU POSSESS AN INNER STRENGTH THAT SURPASSES YOUR OWN PERCEPTION. YOU ARE CAPABLE OF MORE THAN YOU REALISE.

I HOLD DEEP ADMIRATION FOR THOSE UNKNOWN INDIVIDUALS WHO SELFLESSLY SPREAD JOY AND POSITIVITY TO OTHERS. YOUR ACTS OF KINDNESS INSPIRE ME GREATLY, AND I OFFER MY HUMBLE RESPECT FOR YOUR GENUINE CARE AND CONCERN TOWARDS FELLOW HUMAN BEINGS.

EVERY MOMENT OF ADVERSITY AND HARDSHIP WE HAVE FACED HAS CONTRIBUTED TO SHAPING THE INDIVIDUALS WE HAVE BECOME TODAY. RATHER THAN ALLOWING THESE EXPERIENCES TO BREAK US, THEY HAVE SHAPED US INTO STRONGER, MORE RESILIENT VERSIONS OF OURSELVES.

TO FAMILY, STRANGERS, AND ALL THOSE WHO HAVE PLAYED A ROLE IN OUR LIVES, LET US HOLD ONTO GRATITUDE AND INSPIRATION. LET US EMBRACE THE TRANSFORMATIVE POWER OF LOVE, COMPASSION, AND UNITY, AS WE NAVIGATE THE PATHS THAT LIE AHEAD.

REFERENCES

Adam, T. C., & Epel, E. S. (2007). Stress, eating and the reward system. Physiology & Behavior, 91(4), 449-458.

Algoe, S. B., Haidt, J., & Gable, S. L. (2008). Beyond reciprocity: Gratitude and relationships in everyday life. Emotion, 8(3), 425-429.

Baer, R. A. (2003). Mindfulness training as a clinical intervention: A conceptual and empirical review. Clinical Psychology: Science and Practice, 10(2), 125-143.

Bakker, A. B., Demerouti, E., & Sanz-Vergel, A. I. (2017). Burnout and work engagement: The JD-R approach. Annual Review of Organizational Psychology and Organizational Behavior, 4, 389-411.

Baumeister, R. F., Heatherton, T. F., & Tice, D. M. (1994). Losing control: How and why people fail at self-regulation. Academic Press.

Beck, A. T., Rush, A. J., Shaw, B. F., & Emery, G. (2021). Cognitive therapy of depression. Guilford Press.

Beck, J. S. (2011). Cognitive behavior therapy: Basics and beyond. Guilford Press.

Bernstein, E. E., & McNally, R. J. (2017). Relaxation-induced anxiety: Mechanisms and theoretical implications. Behaviour Research and Therapy, 97, 220-230.

Bishop, S. R., et al. (2004). Mindfulness: A proposed operational definition. Clinical Psychology: Science and Practice, 11(3), 230-241.

Bishop, S. R., Lau, M., Shapiro, S., Carlson, L., Anderson, N. D., Carmody, J., ... & Devins, G. (2004). Mindfulness: A proposed operational definition. Clinical Psychology: Science and Practice, 11(3), 230-241.

Boyke, J., Driemeyer, J., Gaser, C., Büchel, C., & May, A. (2008). Training-induced brain structure changes in the elderly. Journal of Neuroscience, 28(28), 7031-7035.

Brackett, M. A., et al. (2011). Emotional intelligence in the classroom: Skill-based training for teachers and students. In J. Ciarrochi, J. P. Forgas, & J. D. Mayer (Eds.), Emotional Intelligence in Everyday Life (2nd ed., pp. 272-293). Psychology Press.

Brown, K. W., & Ryan, R. M. (2003). The benefits of being present: mindfulness and its role in psychological well-being. Journal of Personality and Social Psychology, 84(4), 822-848.

Carlson, L. E., Doll, R., Stephen, J., Faris, P., Tamagawa, R., Drysdale, E., ... & Speca, M. (2019). Randomized controlled trial of mindfulness-based cancer recovery versus supportive expressive group therapy among distressed breast cancer survivors (MINDSET): Long-term follow-up results. Psycho-Oncology, 28(12), 2422-2429.

Chambers, R., Gullone, E., & Allen, N. B. (2009). Mindful emotion regulation: An integrative review. Clinical Psychology Review, 29(6), 560-572.

Clark, S. C., Michel, J. S., Stevens, G. W., Howell, J. W., & Scruggs, R. S. (2016). Work-family boundary profiles: Antecedents and outcomes. Journal of Vocational Behavior, 94, 68-82.

Cohen, S., Janicki-Deverts, D., Doyle, W. J., Miller, G. E., Frank, E., Rabin, B. S., & Turner, R. B. (2019). Chronic stress, glucocorticoid receptor resistance, inflammation, and disease risk. Proceedings of the National Academy of Sciences, 116(22), 11100-11105.

Creswell, J. D. (2017). Mindfulness interventions. Annual Review of Psychology, 68, 491-516.

Csikszentmihalyi, M. (1990). Flow: The psychology of optimal experience. Harper & Row.

Davidson, R. J., & Begley, S. (2013). The emotional life of your brain: How its unique patterns affect the way you think, feel, and live-and how you can change them. Penguin.

Draganski, B., Gaser, C., Busch, V., Schuierer, G., Bogdahn, U., & May, A. (2004). Changes in grey matter induced by training. Nature, 427(6972), 311-312.

Dweck, C. S. (2006). Mindset: The new psychology of success. Random House.

Ekman, P., & Friesen, W. V. (1971). Constants across cultures in the face and emotion. Journal of Personality and Social Psychology, 17(2), 124-129.

Emmons, R. A., & McCullough, M. E. (2003). Counting blessings versus burdens: an experimental investigation of gratitude and subjective well-being in daily life. Journal of Personality and Social Psychology, 84(2), 377-389.

Epel, E. S., Crosswell, A. D., Mayer, S. E., Prather, A. A., Slavich, G. M., Puterman, E., & Mendes, W. B. (2018). More than a feeling: A unified view of stress measurement for population science. Frontiers in Neuroendocrinology, 49, 146-169.

Epel, E. S., Puterman, E., Lin, J., Blackburn, E. H., Lum, P. Y., Beckmann, N. D., ... & Wolkowitz, O. M. (2018). Meditation and vacation effects have an impact on disease-associated molecular phenotypes. Translational Psychiatry, 8(1), 1-13.

Fredrickson, B. L. (2009). Positivity: Top-notch research reveals the 3-to-1 ratio that will change your life. Harmony.

Fredrickson, B. L. (2013). Positive emotions broaden and build. In Advances in Experimental Social Psychology (Vol. 47, pp. 1-53). Academic Press.

Fresco, D. M., et al. (2007). Initial psychometric properties of the experiences questionnaire: validation of a self-report measure of decentering. Behavior Therapy, 38(3), 234-246.

Gable, S. L., & Haidt, J. (2005). What (and why) is positive psychology? Review of General Psychology, 9(2), 103-110.

Goldin, P. R., & Gross, J. J. (2010). Effects of mindfulness-based stress reduction (MBSR) on emotion regulation in social anxiety disorder. Emotion, 10(1), 83-91.

Gotink, R. A., et al. (2016). 8-week Mindfulness Based Stress Reduction induces brain changes similar to traditional long-term meditation practice - A systematic review. Brain and Cognition, 108, 32-41.

Gross, J. J. (1998). The emerging field of emotion regulation: An integrative review. Review of General Psychology, 2(3), 271-299.

Gu, J., Strauss, C., Bond, R., & Cavanagh, K. (2015). How do mindfulness-based cognitive therapy and mindfulness-based stress reduction improve mental health and wellbeing? A systematic review and meta-analysis of mediation studies. Clinical Psychology Review, 37, 1-12.

Hasenkamp, W., et al. (2012). Mind wandering and attention during focused meditation: A fine-grained temporal analysis of fluctuating cognitive states. NeuroImage, 59(1), 750-760.

Hayes, S. C., et al. (2006). Acceptance and commitment therapy: model, processes and outcomes. Behaviour Research and Therapy, 44(1), 1-25.

Hayes, S. C., Luoma, J. B., Bond, F. W., Masuda, A., & Lillis, J. (2006). Acceptance and commitment therapy: Model, processes, and outcomes. Behaviour Research and Therapy, 44(1), 1-25.

Hayes, S. C., Pistorello, J., & Levin, M. E. (2012). Acceptance and commitment therapy as a unified model of behavior change. The Counseling Psychologist, 40(7), 976-1002.

Hofmann, S. G., Asnaani, A., Vonk, I. J., Sawyer, A. T., & Fang, A. (2012). The efficacy of cognitive-behavioral therapy: A review of meta-analyses. Cognitive Therapy and Research, 36(5), 427-440.

Hofmann, S. G., Sawyer, A. T., Witt, A. A., & Oh, D. (2010). The effect of mindfulness-based therapy on anxiety and depression: A meta-analytic review. Journal of Consulting and Clinical Psychology, 78(2), 169-183.

Hoge, E. A., Bui, E., Marques, L., Metcalf, C. A., Morris, L. K., Robinaugh, D. J., . . . Simon, N. M. (2018). Randomized controlled trial of mindfulness meditation for generalized anxiety disorder: Effects on anxiety and stress reactivity. Journal of Clinical Psychiatry, 74(8), 786-792.

Holmes, E. A., & Mathews, A. (2010). Mental imagery and emotion: A special relationship? Emotion Review, 2(4), 320-329.

Holt-Lunstad, J., Robles, T. F., & Sbarra, D. A. (2017). Advancing social connection as a public health priority in the United States. American Psychologist, 72(6), 517-530.

Hölzel, B. K., Carmody, J., Vangel, M., Congleton, C., Yerramsetti, S. M., Gard, T., & Lazar, S. W. (2011). Mindfulness practice leads to increases in regional brain grey matter density. Psychiatry Research: Neuroimaging, 191(1), 36-43.

Hölzel, B. K., et al. (2011). Mindfulness practice leads to increases in regional brain grey matter density. Psychiatry Research, 191(1), 36-43.

Hölzel, B. K., Lazar, S. W., Gard, T., Schuman-Olivier, Z., Vago, D. R., & Ott, U. (2011). How does mindfulness meditation work? Proposing mechanisms of action from a conceptual and neural perspective. Perspectives on Psychological Science, 6(6), 537-559.

Jazaieri, H., Lee, I. A., McGonigal, K., Jinpa, T., Doty, J. R., Gross, J. J., & Goldin, P. R. (2018). A wandering mind is a less caring mind: Daily experience sampling during compassion meditation training. Journal of Positive Psychology, 13(1), 57-66.

Jerath, R., Edry, J. W., Barnes, V. A., & Jerath, V. (2015). Physiology of long pranayamic breathing: Neural respiratory elements may provide a mechanism that explains how slow deep breathing shifts the autonomic nervous system. Medical Hypotheses, 84(2), 87-88.

Jevning, R., Wallace, R. K., & Beidebach, M. (1992). The physiology of meditation: A review. A wakeful hypometabolic integrated response. Neuroscience & Biobehavioral Reviews, 16(3), 415-424.

Jha, A. P., Krompinger, J., & Baime, M. J. (2007). Mindfulness training modifies subsystems of attention. Cognitive, Affective, & Behavioral Neuroscience, 7(2), 109-119.

Kabat-Zinn, J., et al. (1992). Effectiveness of a meditation-based stress reduction program in the treatment of anxiety disorders. The American Journal of Psychiatry, 149(7), 936-943.

Kahneman, D., & Tversky, A. (1979). Prospect theory: An analysis of decision under risk. Econometrica, 47(2), 263-291.

Karim, A. A., & Koles, Z. J. (2018). Involuntary motor activity in mental tasks: Effects of age, task type and imagery vividness. Acta Neurobiologiae Experimentalis, 78(4), 318-326.

Kashdan, T. B., Biswas-Diener, R., & King, L. A. (2008). Reconsidering happiness: The costs of distinguishing between hedonics and eudaimonia. Journal of Positive Psychology, 3(4), 219-233.

Kashdan, T. B., et al. (2014). Experiential avoidance as a generalized psychological vulnerability: Comparisons with coping and emotion regulation strategies. Behaviour Research and Therapy, 51(12), 832-840.

Keng, S. L., Smoski, M Hoge, E. A., Bui, E., Marques, L., Metcalf, C. A., Morris, L. K., Robinaugh, D. J., ... & Simon, N. M. (2018). Randomised controlled trial of mindfulness meditation for generalised anxiety disorder: effects on anxiety and stress reactivity. Journal of Clinical Psychiatry, 79(6), 17m11967.

Keng, S. L., Smoski, M. J., & Robins, C. J. (2011). Effects of mindfulness on psychological health: A review of empirical studies. Clinical Psychology Review, 31(6), 1041-1056.

Khoury, B., et al. (2013). Mindfulness-based stress reduction for healthy individuals: A meta-analysis. Journal of Psychosomatic Research, 78(6), 519-528.

Khoury, B., Lecomte, T., Fortin, G., Masse, M., Therien, P., Bouchard, V., . . . Hofmann, S. G. (2015).

Killingsworth, M. A., & Gilbert, D. T. (2010). A wandering mind is an unhappy mind. Science, 330(6006), 932.

Kok, B. E., Coffey, K. A., Cohn, M. A., Catalino, L. I., Vacharkulksemsuk, T., Algoe, S. B., Brantley, M., & Fredrickson, B. L. (2013). How positive emotions build physical health: Perceived positive social connections account for the upward spiral between positive emotions and vagal tone. Psychological Science, 24(7), 1123-1132.

Kosslyn, S. M., Ganis, G., & Thompson, W. L. (2001). Neural foundations of imagery. Nature Reviews Neuroscience, 2(9), 635-642.

Kosslyn, S. M., Thompson, W. L., & Ganis, G. (2006). The case for mental imagery. Oxford University Press.

Kraft, T. L., & Pressman, S. D. (2012). Grin and bear it: The influence of manipulated facial expression on the stress response. Psychological Science, 23(11), 1372-1378.

Krejtz, I., Nezlek, J. B., Michnicka, A., Holas, P., Rusanowska, M., & Wojciszke, B. (2016). The Experience of Gratitude and Positive Health Outcomes. Journal of Happiness Studies, 17(1), 333-349.

Kristeller, J. L., & Wolever, R. Q. (2011). Mindfulness-based eating awareness training for treating binge eating disorder: The conceptual foundation. Eating Disorders, 19(1), 49-61.

Kushlev, K., Dunn, E. W., & Norton, M. I. (2018). Can experiencing uncertainty improve well-being? The influence of anticipatory thinking about future events on affective forecasts and life satisfaction. Emotion, 18(3), 411-421.

Lazar, S. W., Kerr, C. E., Wasserman, R. H., Gray, J. R., Greve, D. N., Treadway, M. T., ... & Fischl, B. (2005). Meditation experience is associated with increased cortical thickness. Neuroreport, 16(17), 1893-1897.

Lazarus, R. S. (1991). Progress on a cognitive-motivational-relational theory of emotion. American Psychologist, 46(8), 819-834.

LeDoux, J. E. (2012). Rethinking the emotional brain. Neuron, 73(4), 653-676.

Lerner, J. S., Li, Y., Valdesolo, P., & Kassam, K. S. (2015). Emotion and decision making. Annual Review of Psychology, 66, 799-823.

Lutz, A., Jha, A. P., Dunne, J. D., & Saron, C. D. (2015). Investigating the phenomenological matrix of mindfulness-related practices from a neurocognitive perspective. American Psychologist, 70(7), 632-658.

Lyubomirsky, S., Dickerhoof, R., Boehm, J. K., & Sheldon, K. M. (2011). Becoming happier takes both a will and a proper way: An experimental longitudinal intervention to boost well-being. Emotion, 11(2), 391-402.

Lyubomirsky, S., Sheldon, K. M., & Schkade, D. (2005). Pursuing happiness: The architecture of sustainable change. Review of General Psychology, 9(2), 111-131.

Ma, X., Yue, Z. Q., Gong, Z. Q., Zhang, H., Duan, N. Y., Shi, Y. T., ... & Li, Y. F. (2017). The effect of diaphragmatic breathing on attention, negative affect, and stress in healthy adults. Frontiers in Psychology, 8, 874.

Mandolesi, L., Polverino, A., Montuori, S., Foti, F., Ferraioli, G., Sorrentino, P., & Sorrentino, G. (2018). Effects of physical exercise on cognitive functioning and well-being: Biological and psychological benefits. Frontiers in Psychology, 9, 509.

Maslach, C., Schaufeli, W. B., & Leiter, M. P. (2001). Job burnout. Annual Review of Psychology, 52(1), 397-422.

Mauss, I. B., et al. (2005). Making sense of it: the meaning of negative emotions in an integrative perspective. In L. F. Barrett, P. M. Niedenthal, & P. Winkielman (Eds.), Emotion and Consciousness (pp. 301-331). Guilford Press.

McEwen, B. S. (2007). Physiology and neurobiology of stress and adaptation: Central role of the brain. Physiological Reviews, 87(3), 873-904.

Mindfulness-based therapy: A comprehensive meta-analysis. Clinical Psychology Review, 33, 763-771.

Moskowitz, J. T., Epel, E. S., & Acree, M. (2020). Positive effects uniquely predict lower risk of mortality in people with diabetes. Health Psychology, 39(10), 886-893.

Moss, M., Cook, J., Wesnes, K., & Duckett, P. (2006). Aromas of rosemary and lavender essential oils differentially affect cognition and mood in healthy adults. International Journal of Neuroscience, 113(1), 15-38.

Neff, K. D. (2003). Development and validation of a scale to measure self-compassion. Self and Identity, 2(3), 223-250.

Neff, K. D. (2011). Self-compassion: The proven power of being kind to yourself. HarperCollins.

Niemiec, R. M. (2013). Mindfulness and character strengths: A practical guide to flourishing. Hogrefe Publishing.

O'Reilly, J. D. (2014). The Effects of Mindful Eating on Weight Management. Obesity, 22(6), 1348-1355.

Oettingen, G., Pak, H. J., & Schnetter, K. (2016). Self-regulation of goal pursuit. In Advances in Experimental Social Psychology (Vol. 54, pp. 143-206). Academic Press.

Oldham-Cooper, R. E., Hardman, C. A., Nicoll, C. E., Rogers, P. J., & Brunstrom, J. M. (2011). Playing a computer game during lunch affects fullness, memory for lunch, and later snack intake. The American Journal of Clinical Nutrition, 93(2), 308-313.

Oliver, G., & Wardle, J. (1999). Perceived effects of stress on food choice. Physiology & Behavior, 66(3), 511-515.

Ong, A. D., Rothstein, J. D., & Uchino, B. N. (2009). Loneliness accentuates age differences in cardiovascular responses to social evaluative threat. Psychology and Aging, 24(2), 492-504.

Ostafin, B. D., Chawla, N., & Bowen, S. (2012). Intensive mindfulness training and the reduction of psychological distress: A preliminary study. Cognitive and Behavioral Practice, 19(2), 303-312.

Parker, S. K., Bindl, U. K., & Strauss, K. (2010). Making things happen: A model of proactive motivation. Journal of Management, 36(4), 827-856.

Parks, A. C., Schueller, S. M., & Tasimi, A. (2014). Increasing happiness in the general population: Empirically supported self-help? Journal of Happiness Studies, 15(1), 144-166.

Pearson, J., Naselaris, T., Holmes, E. A., & Kosslyn, S. M. (2015). Mental imagery: Functional mechanisms and clinical applications. Trends in Cognitive Sciences, 19(10), 590-602.

Prescott, J. (2004). Flavour as a psychological construct: Implications for perceiving and measuring the sensory qualities of foods. Food Quality and Preference, 15(7-8), 549-557.

Ricard, M., & Lutz, A. (2014). The Art of Meditation: Four Classic Meditative Techniques Adapted for Modern Life. Hay House.

Rimes, K. A., & Wingrove, J. (2011). Mindfulness-based cognitive therapy for people with chronic fatigue syndrome still experiencing excessive fatigue after cognitive behaviour therapy: A pilot randomized study. Clinical Psychology & Psychotherapy, 18(3), 264-275.

Rosenkranz, M. A., Davidson, R. J., Maccoon, D. G., Sheridan, J. F., Kalin, N. H., & Lutz, A. (2013). A comparison of mindfulness-based stress reduction and an active control in modulation of neurogenic inflammation. Brain, Behavior, and Immunity, 27(1), 174-184.

Salovey, P., & Mayer, J. D. (1990). Emotional intelligence. Imagination, Cognition and Personality, 9(3), 185-211.

Schaufeli, W. B., Bakker, A. B., & Van Rhenen, W. (2009). How changes in job demands and resources predict burnout, work engagement, and sickness absenteeism. Journal of Organizational Behavior, 30(7), 893-917.

Scholz, J., Klein, M. C., Behrens, T. E., & Johansen-Berg, H. (2009). Training induces changes in white-matter architecture. Nature Neuroscience, 12(11), 1370-1371.

Sharma, D., Sharma, A., & Sharma, S. (2017). Role of deep breathing in stress and anger management. Journal of Dental and Allied Sciences, 6(2), 70-73.

Sheldon, K. M., & Elliot, A. J. (1999). Goal striving, need satisfaction, and longitudinal well-being: The self-concordance model. Journal of Personality and Social Psychology, 76(3), 482-497.

Siegel, D. J. (2010). The mindful brain: Reflection and attunement in the cultivation of well-being. WW Norton & Company.

Sirois, F. M., & Kitner, R. (2015). Less adaptive or more maladaptive? A meta-analytic investigation of procrastination and coping. European Journal of Personality, 29(4), 433-444.

Slavich, G. M. (2016). Life stress and health: A review of conceptual issues and recent findings. Teaching of Psychology, 43(4), 346-355.

Smith, K. E., Schüz, B., Ode, S., & Galloway, G. (2019). Better cognitive control: An adaptive function of self-reported emotion awareness. Cognition and Emotion, 33(2), 343-354.

Sonnentag, S. (2018). Recovery from work-related stress: A review and research agenda. Applied Psychology, 67(1), 1-35.

Stanczyk, N., Bolinski, F., Canada, B., & Graves, R. (2019). The effectiveness of relaxation on adult patients undergoing magnetic resonance imaging: An evidence-based practice project. Journal of Radiology Nursing, 38(2), 103-107.

Tang, Y. Y., et al. (2015). The neuroscience of mindfulness meditation. Nature Reviews Neuroscience, 16(4), 213-225.

Tang, Y. Y., Hölzel, B. K., & Posner, M. I. (2015). The neuroscience of mindfulness meditation. Nature Reviews Neuroscience, 16(4), 213-225.

Tang, Y. Y., Ma, Y., Wang, J., Fan, Y., Feng, S., Lu, Q., ... & Posner, M. I. (2007). Short-term meditation training improves attention and self-regulation. Proceedings of the National Academy of Sciences, 104(43), 17152-17156.

Tang, Y. Y., Tang, R., & Posner, M. I. (2015). Mindfulness meditation improves emotion regulation and reduces drug abuse. Drug and Alcohol Dependence, 163, S13-S18.

Tangney, J. P., Baumeister, R. F., & Boone, A. L. (2004). High self-control predicts good adjustment, less pathology, better grades, and interpersonal success. Journal of Personality, 72(2), 271-324.

Tonello, L., Rapp Ricciardi, M., Brondino, M., Croce, E., Ricci, L., & Rezzonico, N. (2019). Work-life balance: The role of work engagement and self-efficacy. Frontiers in Psychology, 10, 2053.

Trougakos, J. P., Hideg, I., Cheng, B. H., & Beal, D. J. (2008). Lunch breaks unpacked: The role of autonomy as a moderator of recovery during lunch. Academy of Management Journal, 51(1), 131-146.

Vago, D. R., & Silbersweig, D. A. (2012). Self-awareness, self-regulation, and self-transcendence (S-ART): A framework for understanding the neurobiological mechanisms of mindfulness. Frontiers in Human Neuroscience, 6, 296.

Van Boven, L., & Ashworth, L. (2007). Looking forward, looking back: anticipatory and retrospective judgments of happiness in college students. Cognition & Emotion, 21(8), 1-22.

Verschure, P. F., Pennartz, C. M., & Pezzulo, G. (2014). The why, what, where, when and how of goal-directed choice: neuronal and computational principles. Philosophical Transactions of the Royal Society B: Biological Sciences, 369(1655), 20130483.

Whillans, A. V., Dunn, E. W., Smeets, P., Bekkers, R., & Norton, M. I. (2017). Time, money, and happiness: How does putting a price on time affect our ability to smell the roses? Social Psychological and Personality Science, 8(6), 651-659.

Wood, J. V., Elaine Perunovic, W. Q., & Lee, J. W. (2009). Positive self-statements: Power for some, peril for others. Psychological Science, 20(7), 860-866.

Zeidan, F., Johnson, S. K., Diamond, B. J., David, Z., & Goolkasian, P. (2010). Mindfulness meditation improves cognition: Evidence of brief mental training. Consciousness and Cognition, 19(2), 597-605.

Zeidan, F., Vago, D. R., & Zeidan, R. K. (2021). Mindfulness meditation-based pain relief: A mechanistic account. Annals of the New York Academy of Sciences, 1486(1), 50-67.

Zelazo, P. D., & Lyons, K. E. (2012). The potential benefits of mindfulness training in early childhood: a developmental social cognitive neuroscience perspective. Child Development Perspectives, 6(2), 154-160.

Printed in Great Britain
by Amazon

45117794R00142